Illustrated

CADILLAC
BUYER'S ★ GUIDE℠

Motorbooks International Illustrated Buyer's Guide Series

Illustrated

CADILLAC
BUYER'S ★ GUIDE™

Richard M. Langworth

Motorbooks International
Publishers & Wholesalers

First published in 1993 by Motorbooks
International Publishers & Wholesalers, PO Box
2, 729 Prospect Avenue, Osceola, WI 54020 USA

Motorbooks International books are also
available at discounts in bulk quantity for
industrial or sales-promotional use. For details
write to Special Sales Manager at the Publisher's
address

Library of Congress Cataloging-in-Publication
Data

   Langworth, Richard M.
     Illustrated Cadillac buyer's guide/Richard
M. Langworth. – – 2nd ed.
     p. cm. – – (Motorbooks International
illustrated buyer's guide series)
     Includes index.
     ISBN 0-87938-744-0
     1. Cadillac automobile – – Purchasing. 2.
Used cars – – Purchasing.
I. Title. II. Series.
TL215.C27L36 1993
629.222'2– –dc20   93-17449

On the front cover: A 1959 Cadillac Sixty-Two
powered by a 390ci V-8 and painted in Gotham
Gold. It is owned by Diane Morrow of Windsor,
California. *David Fetherston*

Printed and bound in The United States of America

Contents

	Introduction	7
	Investment Rating	10
Chapter 1	Sixty-One 1946–47	13
Chapter 2	Sixty-Two 1946–47	17
Chapter 3	Sixty-Special 1946–47	23
Chapter 4	Seventy-Five 1946–49	26
Chapter 5	Sixty-One 1948	30
Chapter 6	Sixty-Two 1948	33
Chapter 7	Sixty-Special 1948	35
Chapter 8	Sixty-One 1949–51	37
Chpater 9	Sixty-Two 1949–53	39
Chapter 10	Sixty-Special 1949–53	47
Chapter 11	Seventy-Five 1950–53	52
Chapter 12	Eldorado 1953	56
Chapter 13	Sixty-Two 1954–56	62
Chapter 14	Eldorado 1954–55	67
Chapter 15	Sixty-Special 1954–56	71
Chapter 16	Seventy-Five 1954–67	74
Chapter 17	Sixty-Two 1957–58	81
Chapter 18	Eldorado 1957–58	86
Chapter 19	Eldorado Brougham 1957–58	89
Chapter 20	Sixty-Special 1957–58	94
Chapter 21	Sixty-Two, DeVille 1959–60	96
Chapter 22	Eldorado 1959–60	101
Chapter 23	Eldorado Brougham 1959–60	104
Chapter 24	Sixty-Special 1959–60	106
Chapter 25	Sixty-Two, DeVille 1961–64	108
Chapter 26	Eldorado 1961–66	113
Chapter 27	Sixty-Special 1961–65	115
Chapter 28	Calais, DeVille 1965–70	117
Chapter 29	Sixty-Special 1966–70	121
Chapter 30	Eldorado 1967–70	126
Chapter 31	Fleetwood Seventy-Five 1968–76	133
Chapter 32	Calais, DeVille 1971–76	135
Chapter 33	Sixty Special Fleetwood Brougham, 1971–76	138
Chapter 34	Eldorado 1971–78	141
Chapter 35	Seville 1975–79	147
Chapter 36	DeVille, Fleetwood Limousine, 1977–84 Fleetwood Brougham, 1977–86 Brougham, 1987–92 Fleetwood, 1993	153
Chapter 37	Eldorado 1979–85	159
Chapter 38	Seville 1980–85	162
Chapter 39	Cimarron 1982–88	168
Chapter 40	DeVille, 1985–93 Fleetwood, 1985–92 Sixty-Special, 1987–93	171
Chapter 41	Fleetwood Seventy-Five, 1985–87	176
Chapter 42	Eldorado, Seville, 1986–91	179
Chapter 43	Eldorado, Seville, 1992–93	183
Chapter 44	Allanté 1987–93	186
	Cadillac Ownership	190
	Index	192

Introduction

Cadillac was a relatively slow starter as a collector car, years ago during the original classic car movement, and in more recent times among the "special interest" crowd. The true Classic Car Club Cadillacs (all prewar models except Seventy-Fives through 1949) were spoken for long ago, of course, and there aren't that many Cadillacs from the antique period around. But the postwar models are still—relatively—affordable. And, since Cadillac production soared after the war, they're relatively numerous.

Exactly why Cadillac took so long to start moving in the special interest car class is no more certain than the reasons behind the whims of the people who make up that field. But you can take a few good guesses.

First, Cadillac is not an independent. It lacks the glamorous mass appeal of Packard which, as the only independent postwar luxury car, is far and away the choice of American luxury car collectors. Industry significance, often a vital factor in determining collectibility, is less important here: Far more 1948 Packards are being restored today than 1948 Cadillacs, though the latter figured more importantly in the industry. There is the additional fact of appearance. Cadillac bodies, while of unique proportions, have a family resemblance to other, lesser GM products, and a car's appeal to collectors is often predicated on its looking "different"—even if different means worse, as in the 1948 Packard's case.

While the postwar Cadillac remains among the more attainable makes of its era, we shouldn't conclude that every example is cheap. Convertibles, especially the earlier models, are fetching higher and higher prices all the time. The Eldorado Brougham, in limited supply at release, is even more limited—and desired—today. We also have the unique phenomenon of the 1976 Eldorado convertible, the first instance of a manufacturer building a brand-new "collector item" and touting it as such. (That model has quite deservedly bombed on the collector market, and Cadillac partisans cracked many a smile when a couple of lawyers recently filed a class-action suit against the Division, for "damaging their investment" by again producing convertibles.)

I personally think that "collectibility"—whatever we individually understand that much-abused word to mean—is generally in a downward trend in the case of Cadillac. Between the Richard Nixon and Jimmy Carter eras, for example, we witnessed the downgrading of performance and fuel mileage in a quest for "safety" and "clean air." However desirable those goals may be, one wonders if the sacrifices made in the basic quality of personal transportation improved matters much. Indeed it's been observed that powerplants in Ohio have been spewing junk into the atmosphere for half a century without any evidence of acid rain—and yet we now have a serious problem with it. Said problem began almost simultaneously with the federal mandate for catalytic converters, which spew sulphuric acid into the air. Interesting, isn't it?

Cadillac, being a big, heavy luxury car, suffered more than the average vehicle during what enthusiasts now call the Dark Decade. The cars Cadillac turned out in those days were expensive to buy and run, devilishly complicated, not particularly well built, and oversized in every dimension. We have no trouble visualizing any clean, original 1949 Cadillac sedan being a prized collector item, for example—but can you picture anyone turning handstands over a 1975 DeVille? Maybe you, not me. The cars of the Dark Decade seemed to lose the famous edge that had marked the "Standard of the World" since it wrested the title of choice-of-the-wealthy away from Packard in the late thirties and forties: that spirit of laissez faire extravagance and clever, sound engineering that have always been Cadillac trademarks. To many, the Caddys of the mid-seventies were just things—shapeless, overweight lumps of iron and chrome and plastic that will not be missed when the last one has vanished into the primal mists from whence it came.

And, while the eighties have been a renaissance of sorts for long-suffering American marques like Chrysler, Plymouth, Corvette, Buick and Mercury, they haven't really seemed to do much for Cadillac. With a few distinct exceptions (and I think immediately of the glamorous 1980-85 Seville and the lithe, downsized Eldorado), there haven't been many memorable Cadillacs of late. (About the Cimarron it is best to draw a curtain of silence, lest we suggest that in this non-car and non-Cadillac, a great company has sold its soul to beancounters and extremists. The least they could have done was call it a LaSalle, and spare a proud name from hucksterism.)

My English colleague Graham Robson recently had the effrontery (and some fanatics actually called it that) to state last year that Cadillac isn't really a luxury car anymore, and hasn't set any standards in the past twenty-five years. At first glance I questioned that, but the more I thought about it the more I realized that Graham was right. Today's Cadillacs are well built, attractive and posh, alright, but they aren't the all-dominating *grand luxe* carriages they were

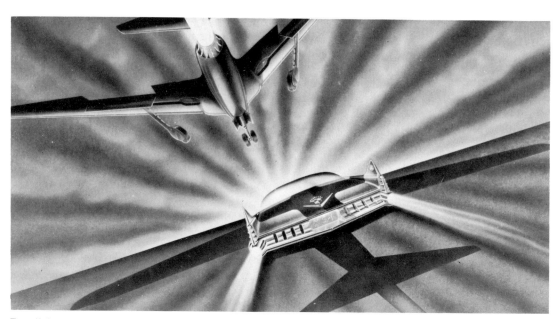

Fanciful rendering from Cadillac Styling Studio, mid-fifties, hints at the aircraft-inspired Cadillac designs since 1948. The plane, of course, is no longer the Lockheed P-38, but a jet!

in the past—represented by the likes of the pre-1950 Seventy-Fives, the 1953 Eldorado, the 1957-58 Eldorado Brougham and the 1967 front-drive coupe. Today there's a whole new level of luxury, way above the Cadillac scale, in the rarified megabuck Mercedes and Rolls-Royce, the limited-production Lagondas for the oil trade, and a host of "replicars," some of which are remarkably good. Cadillac has apparently realized this, since it will launch in 1986 an open two-seater called the Callisto to compete head-on (so they say) with the Mercedes-Benz SLs. But glory, it shares one of GM's ugliest bodies in history, and if I had $50,000 to drop I'd drop it on a Bimmer.

As to setting standards, I can't think of any the Standard of the World has put down since the original Eldorado Brougham. The 1967 Eldo shared its technology with the Toronado of 1966; the 1975 Seville, while a notable car, was hardly the first shrink-job, even if GM said it was; full-independent suspension and four-wheel disc brakes are not Cadillac's to claim. About the only standard one can recall Cadillac setting of late was the unlamented V-8-6-4 engine, and they'd really prefer if you forgot that, thank you.

There are definite signs that the gang at Clark Avenue has concluded that such deviations as the Cimarron are mistakes, and that Cadillacs of the late eighties will again strive to become the exclusive and overwhelming top choice among people who don't write in the upper half of their checkbooks. I hope they will succeed. They have a great heritage. And with Packard long dead, Imperial recently demised (for the second time) and Lincoln floundering around with styling exercises in hypergrossness, Cadillac is about the only luxury heritage the American industry has left.

It's a happy thing that car collectors can find dozens of examples of truly great Cadillacs from the 1945-70 period (never forgetting the post-1979 Seville). And helping you make the choice that's right for you is what this book is about. I have to thank in particular my friend Bud Juneau, editor of the Cadillac-LaSalle club annual, and his colleagues within the club, for advice and expertise; and Bill Kosfeld and Barbara Harold of Motorbooks International, for rendering my manuscript into a finer state of tune. The only trouble with Motorbooks' Illustrated Buyer's Guide series of books is that it contains too few American subjects. I hope this will start a trend in the other direction.

Richard M. Langworth
Hopkinton, New Hampshire
December 1985

In the eight years since this book was first published, Cadillac collecting has grown apace. I have therefore included not only the cars built since 1985, but those I had originally left out: Fleetwood Broughams, Seventy-fives, Sedan and Coupe DeVille and Calais models from the 1970s and early 1980s. I have also been able to close the Cimarron chapter, and to write both a beginning and (alas) an end to the Allanté chapter. I wish to thank in particular Cadillac collectors Don Frolich (early postwar), Bob Hallada (Eldorado Brougham), Bud Juneau (postwar) and Frank Saglimbeni (1970s models) for their kindness in critiquing and correcting past errors, and Mr. Frolich in particular for his note at the end of Chapter 3. I also thank Michael Dregni, Barbara Harold and the Motorbooks International staff, for giving me the opportunity to add new life to this Buyer's Guide.

R.M.L., MARCH 1993

Investment rating

★★★★★   The top of the collector car line. These Cadillacs represent the fondest dreams of postwar Cadillac collectors, and for most of those people they are likely to remain so. They tend not to be advertised in newspapers or the collector car press, but change hands quietly between knowledgeable owners. They tend usually to be, but are not always, very limited production models, or special permutations of volume models. They represent the highest long-term investment value, but like all blue chips their value rises consistently and slowly. Don't expect one to be worth $20,000 today and $30,000 tomorrow.

★★★★   A relatively scarce model of very high value among collectors, regularly sought after and usually salable, with strong investment potential. These cars are better short-term investments than the ones above, because there is a larger number of people who want them—and can afford them. Not often seen in newspaper ads, but occasionally found in the collector car classifieds. The best sources, however, are still the Cadillac clubs and enthusiasts.

★★★   Excellent value, much easier to find than the above categories, though hardly common. Good investment value over the short- to middle-term. An especially good choice if you plan to do a lot of driving in your collectible Cadillac. This class may contain some "sleepers" that will eventually move up to the class above.

★★   Good cars to drive and enjoy. With Cadillac, this usually means the closed models, particularly the four-door sedans, and the lowest price range—Sixty-One, Calais and the like. It also includes the occasional senior model, if only because supply of these larger Cadillacs far outstrips demand.

★   Common, readily available models of modest or little investment potential. Also, any Cadillac that has been modified or incorrectly restored (though one star doesn't signify that in this book).

In the case of Cadillac, selecting your best investment is largely a matter of simple common sense. The limited production of the 1957-60 Eldorado Broughams puts them in a fairly high position, for example, but other factors come into play that separate 1957-58 from 1959-60: The earlier series was far more unique (compared to volume models) than the 1959-60 series. Convertibles and, to a lesser extent, hardtops (especially two-door hardtops) are inevitably better investments than closed cars, but they are also more difficult to restore—you should look for the best one available.

For the newer cars, generally from 1970 to the present, the ratings reflect more an estimate of potential value than a definite opinion. Cadillacs of the last eight or ten years are generally still depreciating; only when their "used car value" bottoms and they start picking up again will we be able to chart the rapidity of their rise as collectibles. In these cases, the potential buyer should simply consider the age-old rules of car collecting: Open models are preferable to closed models; deluxe versions and special trim packages beat "standard spec" types every time; unique styling treatments (like that of the second-series Seville) probably indicate future collector value.

As with the older Cadillacs, however, the fact that a car is the top of the range does not necessarily mean it will be more valuable than everything else that year: It is really very hard, for example, to sell a big Seventy-Five. The most collectible large Cadillacs are probably the Fleetwood Broughams of the late sixties, but even these will have a depressed market if gasoline ever takes another large price jump. Among the latest cars, the Eldorado and Seville are probably your best bets.

Chapter 1

Sixty-One
1946-47

★★ club coupe (sedanet)
★ four-door sedan

HISTORY

The Sixty-One has been around officially since 1939, though its forebears can be traced to 1934, when Cadillac first began subdividing its V-8s. The name Sixty-One was derived from the first two digits of the post-1935 model designation, but not formalized as a title until 1939. The Sixty-One has always been a slightly detrimmed, cheaper version of an upper-class linemate (the Sixty-Two after the war) except in 1940, when it didn't appear. It was more a price leader than a volume seller after 1945, and is therefore scarcer, model for model, than the Sixty-Two today. Postwar Sixty-Ones came in only two basic body styles: coupe and sedan.

IDENTIFICATION

Wheelbase (126 inches) is three inches shorter than the Sixty-Two. ID plate carries model designation 6107 (coupe) or 6109 (sedan). Plain paneled upholstery on both seats and seatbacks.

1946: Six horizontal grille bars in varying lengths use vertical louvers to form rectangular openings. Rectangular parking lights, rubber stone shields, block-letter fender name, six grille bars, "sombrero" type full wheel covers (when so equipped).

Although labeled a Sixty-One in Cadillac's own photograph, this car is really a Sixty-two (with upright instead of raked-forward "B" pillar): proof that you can never be sure of "factory" photos.

1947: Five horizontal grille bars create larger rectangular openings in grille. Hood medallion crest now extends down to fill a V-shaped chrome ornament. Round parking lights (1946 square type optional). Semi-circular horn ring, stainless steel stone shields, script-type fender nameplates.

PERFORMANCE AND UTILITY

Boasting the ultimate development of the flathead Cadillac V-8, these cars were notably smooth and silent over the road, even at speed. Military experience with predecessors of this engine during World War 2 resulted in important changes by 1945, when Cadillac resumed car production: improved cooling, better rings and bearings, new valve guides and tappet bodies for better durability. Carburetor changes resulted in better acceleration. The Hydra-matic (ostensibly an option though, in fact, almost always fitted) was improved, thanks to stronger front and rear bands, main shaft and rear unit clutch hub. Transmission seals were also better, and the clutch plates were revised.

These were fast, satisfying, high-speed touring cars, easily capable of 100 mph. Writes Roy Schneider, "Legions of Americans discovered in this Cadillac a minimum requirement for service work with maximum smoothness, power and dependability."

Sixty-One (note slanted "B" pillar) carried minor gauges to left of speedometer, while Sixty-Two carried them in a round housing. Sixty-One dash, shared with Seventy-five, dated back to 1941.

The 1946 Sixty-One five-passenger touring sedan is less collectible than its more streamlined club coupe relation, and shares its general shape with all other GM sedans of the period.

Cadillac does not issue photos of the Sixty-One tail end, which differed from the Sixty-Two, above. The Sixty-One deck lid broke higher on the body, with the license plate carried just over the bumper. Also, the Sixty-One deck lid had round corners.

PROBLEM AREAS

Physically, these Cadillacs are highly resistant to the dreaded tinworm. But the potential buyer should check all the usual places: rocker panels, seams between body panels, wheel arches and floors. Sixty-Ones do not feature hydraulic window lifts. Upholstery restoration is possible, but the restorer can preserve the car's value only by matching the original material. Plastic interior bits are prone to cracking, but restoration is possible.

Some owners complain of hard starting. Cures you should consider include poor or undersized (i.e. 12-volt) battery cables, or other resistance sources in the starter current path; undersized battery; too much ignition advance, perhaps from "power-tuning" in lieu of timing light tuneups. (With current high-octane gasoline you can run a pretty big advance without getting pre-ignition in these low-compression engines.) Minor oil burning can be ignored unless smoke is visible, in which case an engine rebuild may be needed.

SUMMARY AND PROSPECTS

Never high in value, the Sixty-One is still

The Sixty-One touring sedan for 1946, with factory two-toning and the identifying round parking lights, which replaced the oblong versions this year. As in 1946, this sedan remained a fastback.

1946-47 Sixty-One
ENGINE
Type: . . . . 8-cylinder 90° V-type L-head, watercooled, cast iron
block and heads
Bore x stroke: . . . . 3.50x4.50 in.
Displacement: . . . . 346.0 ci
Valve operation: . . . . sidevalve
Compression ratio: 7.25:1
Carburetion: . . . . dual-throat downdraft
Bhp: . . . . 150 gross (130 net) at 3600 rpm
CHASSIS AND DRIVETRAIN
Transmission: . . . . 3-speed, Hydra-matic optional
Rear axle ratio: . . . . 3.77:1; with Hydra-matic, 3.36:1
Rear suspension:. .live axle, semi-elliptic springs, lever shocks
Front suspension: . . . . independent, coil springs, tube shocks
GENERAL
Wheelbase: . . . . 126.0 in.
Overall length: . . . . 215.0 in.
Track: . . . . 59 in. front, 63 in. rear
Tire size: 7.00x15
Weight: . . . . 4080-4225 lb.
PERFORMANCE
Acceleration: . . . . 0-60: 13 seconds
Top speed: . . . . 100 mph
Fuel mileage: . . . . 12-20 mpg

a satisfying car to own. Doors, hood and deck clang shut like manhole covers; controls operate with a quality feel and emit solid clicks; radios have a deep, fat sound not found even on the most modern transistor systems. The Sixty-One lacks an open body style, but there is definitely more collector interest in the coupe than the sedan. The 1947 versions, with stainless steel instead of rubber splash guards for rear fenders and a less "busy" grille, tend to look more finished.

PRODUCTION	1946	1947
Model 6107		
club coupe	800	3,395
Model 6109		
four-door sedan	2,200	5,160
Bare chassis	1	1

Chapter 2

Sixty-Two
1946-47

★★★	convertible
★★	club coupe (sedanet)
★	four-door sedan

HISTORY

The first Cadillac Sixty-Two (like the Sixty-One, the name was derived from its first two model digits) arrived in 1940, in place of the temporarily absent Sixty-One. The two lines assumed their one-over-the-other position in the Cadillac range in 1941. Cadillac built more Sixty-Ones than Sixty-Twos in the prewar years, but from 1946 the Sixty-Two led by a large margin, mainly through its popular four-door sedan version. It was also offered in club coupe and convertible forms—the only open Cadillac in these years—but convertible production was relatively low.

Closed models had upgraded interiors from the Sixty-Ones, with the seatbacks partly pleated and four choices of Bedford

Breadwinner of the Cadillac line from the restart of production after the war was the Sixty-Two four-door sedan, a notchback (the Sixty-One four-door was a fastback). Immediately indicative of 1946 model year are the standard rectangular parking lights, six-bar grille and rubber stone shields.

cord or broadcloth upholstery. Convertible interiors were a combination of leather and Bedford cord in black, tan, green, blue or red—any other color is not authentic. (There are examples where the leather has been incorrectly replaced with vinyl, as well as the wrong color.) Through 1964 the Sixty-Two was Cadillac's standard-bearer, the quintessential example of the marque.

IDENTIFICATION

Wheelbase (129 inches) is three inches longer than the Sixty-One. Identification plate carries model designation 6207 (coupe), 6269 (sedan), 6267D (1946 convertible) or 6267 (1947 convertible). Better trim in wider color variety than Sixty-One. Only series with a convertible.

PERFORMANCE AND UTILITY

Mechanically, the Sixty-Two was exactly the same as the Sixty-One except that the convertible model featured hydraulic window lifts. As in the Sixty-One, Hydra-matic was ostensibly optional, nearly always fitted. All remarks concerning performance and engineering of the 1946-47 Sixty-One apply here.

PROBLEM AREAS

The Sixty-Two had the same problems as the 1946-47 Sixty-One, with one addition: hydraulic window lifts in the convertible models. Their electro-hydraulic servos involve a complicated network of rubber lines and cylinders at each window which are susceptible to leaks, particularly if each window

This 1947 Sixty-Two convertible bears sombrero wheel covers, which came into use that year. Its vintage can be determined by the parking lights, set where the foglamps used to be under the headlamps.

is not run up and down regularly to keep the seals wet. Hydraulic fluid should be changed annually. Improved fluids are available for use in lieu of regular fluid and won't damage upholstery or paint. Flush the system annually and carefully watch over the fluid lines and cylinders. In addition, door drainage holes must be kept clean, not only to carry off rainwater, but also to channel out hydraulic fluid when the inevitable leak springs.

The leather upholstery in convertibles needs at least annual applications of Clausen's Rejuvenator Oil. This is a ninety-percent-natural animal oil and far superior to other leather conditioners on the market.

SUMMARY AND PROSPECTS

Until 1953, the Sixty-Two series carried Cadillac's only convertible; since convertibles are far and away the most desirable body style for almost any make, the Sixty-Two is important for collectors. Among closed models, there isn't too much to choose from between the Sixty-One and Sixty-Two, although the latter does have a more posh interior, but the condition of the individual car is most important when selecting a closed 1946-47 Cadillac. The 1947 Sixty-

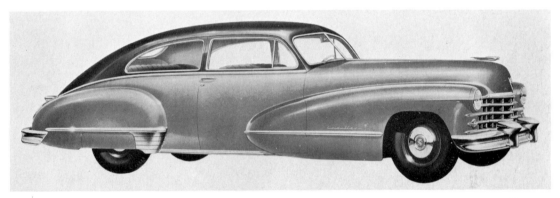

The 1947 Sixty-Two club coupe with factory two-toning but standard small hubcaps. Fender script went from block letters in 1946 to longhand in 1947 on all Cadillacs. A sleek and desirable model.

The 1947 Sixty-Two coupe in a solid color with sombrero wheel covers but still with blackwall tires. The industry only began to reintroduce whitewalls in 1947, and they were still scarce in 1948.

Restorers are cautioned against two-toning cars in color combinations other than those authorized; the Cadillac La Salle Club can be of value in determining authentic combinations. This is a 1947 Sixty-Two five-passenger notchback sedan, factory two-toned.

Two is better looking, thanks to more bright-work and less rubber. The 1947 is also commonly seen with what collectors call the "sombrero" full wheel cover, a handsome stainless steel affair much larger than the corresponding hubcap.

PRODUCTION	1946	1947
Model 6207		
club coupe	2,323	7,245
Model 6267D		
convertible coupe	1,342	6,755
Model 6269		
four-door sedan	14,900	25,834
Bare chassis	1	1

1946-47 Sixty-Two
ENGINE
As per Chapter 1
CHASSIS AND DRIVETRAIN
As per Chapter 1
GENERAL
Wheelbase: . . . . 129.0 in.
Overall length: . . . . 220.0 in.
Track: . . . . 59 in. front, 63 in. rear
Tire size: 7.00x15
Weight: . . . . 4145-4475 lb.
PERFORMANCE
As per Chapter 1

Chapter 3

Sixty-Special
1946-47

★★

The car that made young Bill Mitchell famous back in the late thirties, the Sixty-Special, was in those years an elegant "owner-driver" Cadillac with formal, squarish lines; no running boards; flush-in headlamps; minimal body decoration; distinct delineation of body and greenhouse; and elegant, thin-chrome-banded side windows. With the restyle of 1942, however, the long-wheelbase Sixty-Special became considerably less distinct from the rest of the Cadillac line, and during 1946-47 it stayed that way. It was obviously longer, with a 133-inch wheelbase. It bore the name Fleetwood on the trunk. And it had very luxurious interiors. But it lacked the special style of the pre-1942 Sixty-Special. Priced at $3,100 in 1946 it was twenty-five percent more expensive than the Sixty-Two sedan; yet it remained second only to that model in Cadillac popularity. It remained "coachbuilt," with all the quality of fit and finish that implies.

The 1947 Sixty-Special rode a four-inch-longer wheelbase than the less expensive models, and could be told from them at a glance, with its dummy louvers on the rear roof quarters and thinner window frames.

IDENTIFICATION

Three chrome, vertical louvers at the rear outside roof quarter. Fleetwood script on trunk lid. Brightmetal trim around side window channels. Pleated door panels and other interior trim. Considerable woodgraining inside. (Identification notes on the 1946 and 1947 Sixty-Ones also apply to the 1946 and 1947 Sixty-Specials, respectively.)

PERFORMANCE AND UTILITY

Though powered by the same 150 bhp, 346 cid flathead V-8 as the Sixty-One and Sixty-Two, the Sixty-Special was considerably longer and up to 200 pounds heavier than the smaller sedans; as a result it was less lively and less fun to drive, although a shade more comfortable, particularly for back-seat passengers. For a sedan, the lines were better balanced than the smaller models, thanks to four to seven more inches of wheelbase. Fuel consumption was marginally higher, and handling clumsier. Compared to the Sixty-Two, this car was built for more sedate, quiet motoring.

PROBLEM AREAS

The Sixty-Special has the same problems with rust, upholstery, the V-8 engine and the Hydra-matic as the Sixty-One and Sixty-Two. In addition, interior restoration

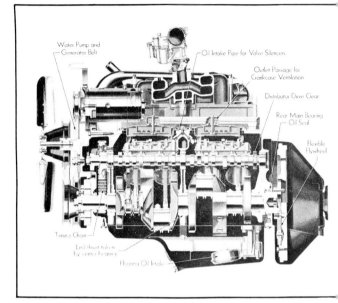

Powering all Cadillacs through 1948, the respected flathead V-8 was a venerable component of the cars' luxury package—smooth and reliable, it's one of the Cadillac enthusiast's favorite engines.

Like other 1946 models, the Sixty-Special can be told from the 1947 by its rectangular foglamps under the headlamps, block lettering on fenders and rubber rear fender stoneguard. (Factory artwork.)

costs are higher: There is more woodgraining, which can rarely be restored except by an expert; and there are more luxury appointments, such as upholstery and carpets. A very clean interior can be a definite plus when shopping for one of these cars.

SUMMARY AND PROSPECTS

This car has more "presence" than the Sixty-One and Sixty-Two four-door sedans, and is not often seen despite its fairly high production. The Sixty-Special, nevertheless, falls into a crack among collectible postwar Cadillacs. It isn't as all-out splendid as the big Seventy-Fives or as sporty and lively as the Sixty-Twos. Also, it tends to be eclipsed by the far more glamorous 1948 and later Sixty-Special models.

It is difficult to rate this car higher than other four-door sedans of the same period. It is a fairly good buy although, car for car, the price of a Sixty-Special is higher than that of a Sixty-One or Sixty-Two four-door sedan.

PRODUCTION	1946	1947
Model 6069		
four-door sedan	5,700	8,500

1946-47 Sixty-Special
ENGINE
As per Chapter 1
CHASSIS AND DRIVETRAIN
As per Chapter 1
GENERAL
Wheelbase: .... 133.0 in.
Overall length: .... 224.0 in.
Track: .... 59 in. front, 63 in. rear
Tire size: 7.00x15
Weight: .... 4370-4420 lb.
PERFORMANCE
As per Chapter 1

An example of how artists of the day stretched their car portraits to give a more streamlined impression is this rendering of a 1947 two-tone Sixty-Special. Compare it to photos of actual cars.

Collector Don Frolich comments: "Although it did not have the special style of the 1941 Sixty-Special, the early postwar version was quite distinct in its way—despite the poor job Cadillac brochures did in illustrating its differences. At 133 inches of wheelbase (the 1941 had only 126 inches) this was clearly an 'owner-driver' Cadillac, and its ride quality was superb. The panel behind the front seat was fixed, independent of seat position, like a formal car with division glass—in 1941 it had been just a regular seatback. The pillar between front and rear door windows is wider and the chromed door trim, and rain gutters separate the post visually from the doors. The rear window is smaller, creating the closed rear quarter impression of a formal body. The roof stamping was unique, though the deck and rear quarter panels were interchangeable with the Sixty-Two. The 1946-47 60S gave all its extra wheelbase to the rear seat passengers, while in the more highly regarded 1948 and later versions, the passengers have to ride in the trunk if they want to enjoy the space benefits of the extra wheelbase, because that's where those seven inches went! The post-1947 silhouette was not an aesthetic improvement and the later interior decal trim and dash were not even close to those of 1946-47. I think collectors are missing the boat by ignoring these cars."

Chapter 4

Seventy-Five
1946-49

★★★★ Fleetwood coachwork
[Classic]
★★★★ Special coachwork

HISTORY

The original Godfather car, the handsome and stately Seventy-Five served Cadillac so well in 1946-47 that the old body style was kept for 1948-49 models. This body stemmed from 1940, with its obviously prewar pontoon fenders, upright grille and abbreviated, rounded trunk lid. An all-new tailfinned design was applied to all junior models in 1948, but the Seventy-Five was so beautifully built, and so well accepted by the wealthy, that its postwar restyling was put off until the 1950 model year.

This series also enjoyed the widest variety of Cadillac body styles, although the list was truncated by prewar standards: There were five- and seven-passenger sedans, business sedans, imperials, a nine-passenger business imperial, and a large number of long-wheelbase chassis supplied to hearse and ambulance builders as well as to specialists like Derham of Rosemount, Pennsylvania, and

The regal 1946 Seventy-Five in its basic five-passenger touring sedan form. Note stainless steel running boards. This model was essentially un-changed through 1949. Note taillamp detail differences from less expensive models.

Maurice Schwartz of Pasadena, California.

After 1948, the Seventy-Five was distinctly dated, but it was so beautifully built, imposing and luxurious that nobody seemed to mind, and it handily outsold the comparable Packards every year.

IDENTIFICATION

Hydraulic window lifts standard from 1947. Much longer, larger and heavier than any other Cadillacs. Only models with prewar styling from 1948. Stainless steel, full-length running boards every year.

1946-47: Differences same as 1946-47 Sixty-Ones.

1948: New, drum-type speedometer.

1949: Much smaller instrument cluster recessed into top of dashboard; large speedometer flanked by shorter auxiliary gauges.

PERFORMANCE AND UTILITY

Undoubtedly a handful to drive, and certainly no car for gymkhana work, these Seventy-Fives remain today what they were in their time: expensive to operate, offering a high degree of luxury for the money you spend to keep them on the road. However, they are by no means fast (with no change in powerplant, they outweigh smaller Cadillacs by up to 780 pounds), and they're quite thirsty. They may also pose size problems for many garages, especially in their monu-

The Superior funeral service car mounted on the 1947 Seventy-Five chassis for commercial vehicles, with a wheelbase of 163 inches. Cadillac dominated the postwar funeral-car business.

The seven-passenger 1947 Seventy-Five sedan, identifiable through its assist straps in the rear compartment. A minor detail change for 1947 was the grille, which had five instead of six horizontal bars for a lower appearance. This was a common change on all models.

mental, 163-inch-wheelbase commercial form.

PROBLEM AREAS

Mechanically, these cars have the same problems as the smaller Cadillacs, with all the same admonitions regarding hydraulics. The high cost of interior restoration matches that of any 1946-47 Fleetwood Cadillac. Those with bodies other than a Fleetwood pose extreme replacement difficulties, although one supposes the collector who opts for such a custom is prepared to pay whatever it takes to make something from scratch.

SPECIAL COACHWORK

Notable work was done on postwar Seventy-Fives by Derham (convertible sedans, town cars, formals) and by Maurice Schwartz (woody wagons and woody sedans, even one three-passenger "golfer's coupe"). Cadillac supplied many long-wheelbase commercial chassis to such builders as Hess & Eisenhardt, Superior Coach Corporation, Sayers & Scoville, Meteor and Eureka, which

What a difference whitewalls make on these big Seventy-Fives! This is a 1948 model, the model 7519-X five-passenger, of which 225 were sold at close to $5,000. Styling was unchanged from 1947.

Photographed in the Cadillac design studios, this car is labeled a 1948 but may be a 1946 (note script fender letters); or it may be a try at slightly changing the 1948 model through script design.

transformed them into hearses, flower cars, ambulances and rescue vehicles.

SUMMARY AND PROSPECTS

The 1946-49 Cadillac Seventy-Five is one of the few postwar cars that may be certified as a Classic by the Classic Car Club of America, which liberalized its standards to include this model and a very few others several years ago. Such a high standing in the collector community inevitably means these are strong investor vehicles, even more desirable because of their limited production. They are strongly recommended for the Cadillac enthusiasts who like their cars the way Don Corleone preferred them.

1946-49 Seventy-Five
ENGINE
In 1946-48, as per Chapter 1. In 1949:
Type: . . . . 8-cylinder 90° V-type, watercooled, cast iron block and cylinder heads
Bore x stroke: . . . . 3.81x3.63 in.
Displacement: . . . . 331.0 ci
Valve operation: . . . . overhead, pushrod actuated
Compression ratio: 7.5:1
Carburetion: . . . . Carter dual downdraft
Bhp: . . . . 160 gross (133 net) at 3800 rpm
CHASSIS AND DRIVETRAIN
Transmission: . . . . 3-speed, Hydra-matic optional
Rear axle ratio: . . . . 4.27:1; with Hydra-matic, 3.77:1
Rear suspension:. . .live axle, semi-elliptic springs, lever shocks
Front suspension: . . . . independent, coil springs, tube shocks
GENERAL
Wheelbase: . . . . 136.0 in.
Overall length: . . . . 226.0 in.
Track: . . . . 59 in. front, 63 in. rear
Tire size: 7.50x16
Weight: . . . . 4790-4960 lb.
PERFORMANCE
Acceleration: . . . . 0-60: 15 seconds
Top speed: . . . . 95 mph
Fuel mileage: . . . . 10-18 mpg

PRODUCTION	1946	1947	1948	1949
Model 7519				
four-door sedan	150	300	225	220
Model 7523				
sedan 7-pass.	225	890	499	595
Model 7523L				
business sedan 9-pass.	22	135	90	35
Model 7533				
imperial 7-pass.	221	1,005	382	626
Model 7533L				
business imperial 9-pass.	17	80	64	25
Bare chassis	0	3	2	1
Commercial chassis,				
163 in. wheelbase	1,292	2,623	2,067	1,861

Chapter 5

Sixty-One
1948

★★★ club coupe (sedanet) [Milestone] ★★ four-door sedan

HISTORY

The look of the 1948 Sixty-One became a Cadillac trademark and the standard by which all luxury rivals were measured. Designers Bill Mitchell, Harley Earl, Frank Hershey and Art Ross conjured up the tremendously successful 1948 redesign after being inspired by the Lockheed Lightning P-38 pursuit fighter at a secret review during the war. The P-38 bestowed its tail outline on Cadillac's rear end and its engine shroud shape on the front fenders. (On another GM design, the Futuramic Oldsmobile, stylists even built in a functional scoop, exactly like the aircraft.)

The tailfins, Mitchell said, gave definition to the rear of the car for the first time (and far more successfully than Studebaker's drooping posterior). Up front, the traditional grille shape was retained, while the hood, roof and fenderlines were graceful from all angles. Attention was given to the interior, where a huge, ornate drum housing for the instruments was installed. Again, the Sixty-One was the price-leader series, comprising only a coupe and a sedan model.

IDENTIFICATION

Recognizable at a glance. Used a triple row of egg-crate shapes for the grille. Cleaner than the similar Sixty-Two, having no front stoneguards, no brightwork along the rocker panels and no bright flashes under the tail-lamp lenses. Interiors again less elaborate

Telling a Sixty-One from a Sixty-Two became easier in 1948, with the great new postwar body style. Sixty-Ones lacked the second stoneguard behind the front wheels. Two-toned cars used a second color to the beltlines.

than on the Sixty-Two. Wheelbases of both Sixty-One and Sixty-Two are identical at 126 inches.

1948: All-new styling, tailfinned rear fenders carrying upright taillights. Two-bar grille forming three rows of rectangular openings. Round parking lights set into chromed panels curved to match fender leading edges. (With fog lamps, parking lamps were incorporated inside the fog lamps.) The instruments were grouped in a large drum-type housing.

PERFORMANCE AND UTILITY

The 1948 models continued to use the 346 cid flathead V-8, introduced in the 1936 models. The 1948 models seemed to handle better and, since weight was about the same, were no thirstier than their 1946-47 predecessors.

PROBLEM AREAS

Comments applied to 1946-47 models with the flathead V-8 are again appropriate here. The same areas should be checked for rust, though the new body did not create any overt problems in that area. Hydra-matic was fitted to nearly ninety percent of Cadil-

lacs by 1948 and, as with all automatics, it should be carefully checked if it has an uncertain history on the car in question. Optional white or black Tenite plastic steering wheels were prone to cracking, particularly white ones. Sharing of the Fisher C-body between Sixty-Ones and Sixty-Twos means body parts may be readily available.

SUMMARY AND PROSPECTS

As progenitors not only of the tailfin but of a whole school of Cadillac styling, the 1948s probably rank as the most collectible early postwar Cadillacs. They also possess a trait peculiar to many first-year designs: They were the cleanest, by far, of the tail-finned models, which gradually became gaudier and paunchier in response to the taste of the public. The elaborate horseshoe instrument cluster, found only in 1948s, gives them special appeal to collectors. But there is no unanimity of opinion about these last flathead V-8s: Many collectors say they were superior to the ohv 1949 V-8 in smoothness and quiet running, and value a

Unique to the 1948 Cadillac line was the huge, elaborate, drum-type instrument cluster, grouping controls under the wheel. It was replaced by a less costly dash for 1949. This one is from a Sixty-Two.

A 1947 clay model shows the 1948 redesign close to its final form. In production, the rear deck emblem was altered, but the in-built bumper remained, despite its cost of manufacture.

Sixty-One over a 1949 for that reason alone; others say quite the opposite.

Whatever your personal opinion, there is no doubt that the 1948 Sixty-One—particularly the club coupe (sedanet) model—has an important standing with collectors. The Sixty-One sedanet is one of the most sought after Cadillacs of the postwar period. Its handsome shape prefigures the later and dramatic R-type Bentley Continental, which means it's a wonderful-looking car. Its lack of chrome compared to that of the Sixty-Two sedanet renders it more attractive to some collectors.

PRODUCTION	1948
Model 6107 club coupe (sedanet)	3,521
Model 6109 four-door sedan	5,081
Bare chassis	1

1948 Sixty-One
ENGINE
As per Chapter 1
CHASSIS AND DRIVETRAIN
As per Chapter 1
GENERAL
Wheelbase: . . . . 126.0 in.
Overall length: . . . . 213.9 in.
Track: . . . . 59 in. front, 63 in. rear
Tire size: 8.20x15
Weight: . . . . 4068-4150 lb.
PERFORMANCE
As per Chapter 1

The 1948 Sixty-One club coupe or sedanet was perhaps the cleanest, most handsome of the 1948 models. With only 3,521 units produced, it is the rarest model/body style except for Seventy-Fives.

Chapter 6

Sixty-Two
1948

★★★★ convertible [Milestone]
★★★ club coupe (sedanet)
[Milestone]
★★ four-door sedan

HISTORY

The Sixty-Two continued in 1948 to be the standard-bearer for Cadillac, its three body styles accounting for over 34,000 sales. Remarkably, neither closed body had a base price over $3,000, and the convertible could be had for as little as $3,442 (although this was admittedly a pretty exclusive price).

Sixty-Twos again came with a higher standard of interior trim than Sixty-Ones, and this year they were more elaborate on the outside as well. However, there was no exterior script signifying the model—such things were thought gauche in those days.

Despite their good looks, the 1948 fastbacks didn't sell particularly well. Their sales percentage of the Sixty-Two line was 13.9 in 1948, against 18.7 percent the year before.

IDENTIFICATION

Triple, bright bars under taillights, bright rocker panel molding and stoneguards aft of the front wheelwells. Triple row of egg-crates on grille. Horseshoe instrument cluster.

PERFORMANCE AND UTILITY

In addition to better handling, the flathead-powered 1948 models performed better, at GM's Milford test track, than 1949-50 models equipped with the new ohv V-8. According to Cadillac, a stock sedan carrying the equivalent of four passengers ran like a clockwork mouse at 93.3 mph. All Sixty-Twos (and Sixty-Ones) were easily capable of 100 mph. Handling, weight and fuel consumption matched those of the 1948 Sixty-One.

The 1948 Sixty-Two sedanet was a lovely fastback, and is highly sought after by collectors today. Front stoneguard identifies this rendering as a Sixty-Two.

PROBLEM AREAS

The Sixty-Two had the same problems as the Sixty-One in 1948. In addition, restoration costs of Sixty-Two interiors may be higher due to the more elaborate, higher-quality materials used.

SUMMARY AND PROSPECTS

The Sixty-Two was again the only Cadillac model range offering a convertible, and here again car collector preferences show: Though the club coupe is stylistically far more interesting and a more unified design, the open Sixty-Two continues to lead in collector markets. Several price guides (1984) peg a perfect Sixty-Two convertible at a maximum of $15,000, while none quote a 100-point club coupe at over $10,000.

PRODUCTION	1948
Model 6207 club coupe (sedanet)	4,764
Model 6267 convertible coupe	5,450
Model 6269 four-door sedan	23,997
Bare chassis	2

1948 Sixty-Two
ENGINE
As per Chapter 1
CHASSIS AND DRIVETRAIN
As per Chapter 1
GENERAL
Wheelbase: . . . . 126.0 in.
Overall length: . . . . 213.9 in.
Track: . . . . 59 in. front, 63 in. rear
Tire size: 8.20x15
Weight: . . . . 4125-4449 lb.
PERFORMANCE
As per Chapter 1

Probably the most dramatic view of the Sixty-Two sedanet. Another special bit of trim was the triple bar decoration under the taillamp. The rounded dash with drum speedometer was a nice, modern feature.

The Sixty-Two four-door sedan for 1948, least desirable of the series because of its more conventional styling and numbers: Cadillac built 23,977, more than all other 1948 models combined.

Sixty-Special
1948

★★★ four-door sedan

HISTORY

The long-wheelbase owner-driver Fleet-wood continued with all-new postwar styling in 1948. The Sixty-Special retained its 133-inch wheelbase, which looked more impressive than ever, since the Sixty-Two was down to 126 inches. Very formal compared to the junior models, the Sixty-Special featured an elongated trunk and a full-length strip of brightwork under the rockers, which continued on through the fenders to the rear. It also featured a slim dummy scoop (stoneguard) on the leading edge of the rear fenders. The traditional bright chevrons were again applied to the formal, closed rear roof quarters, and the Fleetwood name adorned the trunk. Interiors were colorful combinations of fine fabrics and leather, while a leather-grained decal took the place of woodgraining on the dashboard and door reveal moldings. "When the standard of the automotive world has been so decidedly raised," said one Sixty-Special advertisement, "it should be of interest to everyone."

IDENTIFICATION

Very clean body sides compared to other models. Tall, fake combination stone-guard and dummy air scoop on leading edge of rear fenders is a distinguishing characteristic. Five chrome louvers aft of outside window. Full-length bright strip at bottom of body.

PERFORMANCE AND UTILITY

A remarkable combination of size, luxury and performance, the elegant Sixty-Special

The formal Sixty-Special for 1948 carried a dummy scoop at the leading edge of the rear fenders and traditional "louvers" in the rear roof quarter. As before, its wheelbase was four inches longer than the smaller models.

was the proudest new product of Cadillac for 1948. It weighed only fourteen pounds less than its 1947 counterpart, so performance and fuel mileage were about the same. But the dramatic improvement in its looks has rendered it one of the most important closed Cadillacs of this period. This is a big car for many garages: It's a foot longer (226 inches) than the Sixty-One or Sixty-Two. Smooth and silent in motion, the 1948 Sixty-Special is a tribute to the craftsmen who put it together.

PROBLEM AREAS
Same as 1948 Sixty-One.

SUMMARY AND PROSPECTS
Probably the most desirable of the 1948 closed models, the Sixty-Special is still not outlandishly priced. (One current guide places the Sixty-Special as the lowest priced of *all* 1948 models, including the Sixty-One.

This cannot be accurate because it is a better, far more luxurious car.) If you have the garage space, this is a prime collectible which should appreciate rapidly over the next decade.

PRODUCTION   *1948*
Model 6069 four-door sedan   6,561

1948 Sixty-Special	
ENGINE	
As per Chapter 1	
CHASSIS AND DRIVETRAIN	
As per Chapter 1	
GENERAL	
Wheelbase:	133.0 in.
Overall length:	226.0 in.
Track:	59 in. front, 63 in. rear
Tire size:	8.20x15
Weight:	4356 lb.
PERFORMANCE	
As per Chapter 1	

The extra length of the Sixty-Special is readily apparent in this view of a 1948 model. Inches were added to the rear as well as to the wheelbase; brightmetal was kept to a distinct minimum.

Chapter 8

Sixty-One
1949-51

★★★   club coupe (1949) [Milestone]
★★   club coupe (1950-51)
★ four-door sedan

HISTORY

The Sixty-One continued to plug along at a relatively low sales level in its last few years. Among 1949 models the price leader accounted for about 22,000 sales, and another 27,000 the following year. By late 1950, however, the Sixty-One was destined for phase-out, Cadillac having made the decision to concentrate strictly on improving the Sixty-Two as the great postwar seller's market ebbed away. The Division built only 4,700 Sixty-Ones during the 1951 model year. All these Sixty-Ones featured Cadillac's new overhead valve 331 cid V-8.

IDENTIFICATION

As in 1948, detrimmed compared to the Sixty-Two, lacking the front stoneguards and rocker panel brightmolding. No rear quarter windows.

1949: Lower grille with horizontal bar extending across fenders to wheel openings forming two rows of rectangular openings. The sedan had no rear quarter windows, but the coupe did. Horizontal chrome moldings either side of parking lamps. Less elaborate, shorter instrument panel.

1950: Parking lamps set into grille at either end. Bright strip on forward edge of rear door was grille-type stoneguard. One-

The less elaborate (and less expensive) dashboard which arrived on the 1949 duplicated the established shape of the Cadillac grille. In 1951, warning lights, housed in a deeper odometer area, replaced the two outermost gauges.

All-new overhead valve Cadillac engine powered all 1949 models including the Sixty-One. Owners are divided over the merits of this engine compared to the previous flathead. Many parts for the ohv are as scarce, or scarcer, than similar bits for flatheads.

piece, curved windshield. Coupe deck much shorter than Sixty-Two deck.

1951: Five vertical-sectioned chrome grilles on either side of grille under head-lamps, extending to front wheel openings. Built-in back-up lamps flush below tail-lamps. Hydra-matic shift indicator moved to recess near steering wheel hub. Automatic key-ignition starter.

PERFORMANCE AND UTILITY
Same as 1949-53 Sixty-Two.

PROBLEM AREAS
Same as 1949-53 Sixty-Two.

SUMMARY AND PROSPECTS
Historically, the 1949s are most important for their all-new V-8 engine (see next chapter). Cadillac styling became progressively heavier starting in 1949, and though club coupe Sixty-Ones were offered through 1951, only the 1949 version was particularly outstanding—similar enough to the original 1948 to remain especially handsome. Like other Sixty-Ones the 1949-51 models are less sought after than the Sixty-Twos, and include neither the glamorous new Coupe de Ville hardtop nor the sporty convertible. These cars have much lower investment potential than previous Sixty-One models.

Even the low production of the 1951 vintage does not seem to work in their favor—supply has remained adequate to meet the limited demand.

PRODUCTION	1949	1950	1951
Model 6107			
club coupe	6,409	11,839	2,400
Model 6169			
four-door			
sedan	15,738	14,931	2,300
Bare chassis	1	2	0

1949-51 Sixty-One
ENGINE
Type: . . . . 8-cylinder 90° V-type, watercooled, cast iron block and heads
Bore x stroke: . . . . 3.81x3.63 in.
Displacement: . . . . 331.0 ci
Valve operation: . . . . overhead, pushrod actuated
Compression ratio: 7.5:1
Carburetion: . . . . Carter dual downdraft
Bhp: . . . . 160 gross (133 net) at 3800 rpm
CHASSIS AND DRIVETRAIN
As per Chapter 1. . . . . .Tube-type rear shocks from 1950.
GENERAL
Wheelbase: . . . . 1949: 126.0 in.; 1950-51: 122.0 in.
Overall length: . . . . 1949: 213.9 in.; 1950-51: 211.9 in.
Track: . . . . 59 in. front, 63 in. rear
Tire size: 1949: 8.20x15; 1950: 8.00x15; 1951: 7.60x15
Weight: . . . . 3830 lb.
PERFORMANCE
Acceleration: . . . . 0-60: 13.5 seconds
Top speed: . . . . 100+ mph
Fuel mileage: . . . . 14-22 mpg

Some enthusiasts now prefer detrimmed Sixty-Ones from the 1949-51 period to the more luxurious Sixty-Twos. Although the latter have nicer interiors, the Sixty-One is cleaner on the outside, lacking the brightmetal rocker panel molding and front splash guard. The 1949 sedanet is the most desirable body style and year.

Chapter 9

Sixty-Two
1949-53

★★★★ convertible
★★★★ Coupe de Ville (1949) [Milestone]
★★★ club coupe (1949) [Milestone]
★★★ convertible (1950-53)
★★★ Coupe de Ville (1950-53)
★★ four-door sedan (1949)
★ four-door sedan (1950-53)
★★ club coupe (1950-53)

HISTORY

After the tailfins of 1948, the ohv V-8 of 1949 was Cadillac's second potent punch delivered to the competition, and the final ingredient in its dominance of the postwar luxury car market. The engine, designed by Ed Cole, Jack Gordon and Harry Barr, was the product of ten years' concentrated research and experimentation. The designers' goals: to reduce weight and increase com-

Cadillac archives have this photo labeled "1949 Sixty-One." Actually it is a 1948 Sixty-Two, retouched with the 1949 grille. Things are not always what they seem; even factory photographs should be studied when relying on them for a restoration.

pression to take advantage of forthcoming higher-octane fuels. These dictated the valve arrangement, the short stroke, the wedge-shaped combustion chambers and the famous "slipper" pistons. The latter, developed by Byron Ellis, traveled low between the crankshaft counterweights, allowing for short conn-rods and low reciprocating weight.

Although the new engine displaced fifteen fewer cubic inches than the old flathead, it developed ten percent more horsepower, and was capable of far more than that. It weighed nearly 200 pounds less than its predecessor and had an initial compression of only 7.5:1, which could be raised to as much as 12:1 if high-octane fuel became available. The new ohv V-8 produced more torque and delivered fourteen percent better gas mileage. It was durable and reliable,

though Cadillac collectors did not consider it as smooth a runner as the flathead.

A new entry in the 1949 Sixty-Two series, and a car now avidly sought by collectors, was the handsome Coupe de Ville "hardtop-convertible." Joining the Olds Holiday and Buick Riviera as the first production hardtops in the modern sense, the Coupe de Ville, priced at $3,500, accounted for 2,150 sales in 1949—a higher percentage of the whole than either Holiday or Riviera. By 1953 it was up to nearly 15,000 sales. It was a highly successful combination of the airiness and sportiness of a convertible with the snugness and comfort of a sedan, and it started a trend that dominated the industry by the late fifties.

IDENTIFICATION

1949: Front stoneguards and brightwork

The sedanet remained the outstanding closed Cadillac model in 1949, and the only exterior change was its two-tier (instead of three) grille; far more significant was the new engine.

As in 1948, the Sixty-Two four-door retained its rear quarter windows. Since major collector emphasis is on the sportier body styles, the dignified sedan models can still be found at very reasonable prices.

The factory workers didn't bother to clean up the whitewalls when they photographed this Sixty-Two convertible. Buyers should pay close attention to the soft tops on these models to be sure any replacement work has been patterned after the original style and backlight opening.

rocker panel overlays, with 1948 triple bright strips under the taillights eliminated.

1950: Retained rear quarter windows.

1951: Power windows were standard on convertible and hardtop models. Coupe de Ville script in the rear quarter chrome panel above the belt molding.

1952: Golden Anniversary series, the only junior-line Cadillac series. Broad chrome trim below headlamps. Side scoop styling. Winged emblem mounted in center. V emblem and crest on hood and rear deck broader than before. Dual exhaust ports integral in rear bumpers. Power steering optional on all models.

1953: Again the only junior-line Cadillac series. Bullt-like guards atop bumpers, known as "Dagmars" after the buxom Hollywood star. Parking lights mounted under headlamps. One-piece backlight.

PERFORMANCE AND UTILITY

Like the Sixty-One, the relatively light Sixty-Two could clock 0-60 mph times of around thirteen seconds and could easily top 130 mph, even with Hydra-matic (which became standard in 1950). Driven by Sam and Miles Collier, a 1950 Cadillac finished tenth at Le Mans, a performance unrivaled by any other luxury make. It sped at 120 mph down the Mulsanne Straight and averaged 81.5 mph for the French enduro. Chicago enthusiast Ed Gaylord owned a stickshift 1950 model with a 3.77 rear axle ratio, which he said was faster than the Jaguar XK120 up to 90 mph. The first Cadillacs with a truly modern drivetrain, these are tremendously satisfying, big road cars, capable of handling most modern motoring conditions.

PROBLEM AREAS

Early 1949 ohv V-8s are known for their durability, even after racking up six-figure mileage. However, they are often faulted for hard starting, caused by voltage drop during starting cycle. This may be due to battery connections, ground, starter solenoid connections, or a worn or poorly rebuilt starter. (See also notes on this section in Chapter 1.) Late in the 1949 model year, the V-8 received

Highly desirable Coupe de Ville shared an historic first with Olds Holiday and Buick Riviera as the first mass-volume hardtops, although the de Ville accounted for only 2,150 units in this first year, 1949. Examples are now extremely scarce and bring the very highest prices.

thicker heads to eliminate warping problems in the field, and a changed piston design. if you have starting problems, you may try changing to the later wire loom, or have the valves ground. Also check for water droplets on your crankcase dipstick; this indicates a leaky head, which can cause starting problems. the cure is to be sure there is full compression in each cylinder and to torque the heads to service specs. The last resort is a new starter, but this is rarely the culprit.

From 1950 through 1955, these early nits were worked out, and the 1950-55 V-8s are sweet-running engines. This is ironic, since the 1949 models are by far the most desirable vintage ohvs.

Fewer bugs appeared in the Hydra-matic, but continual use of the V-8's power and torque is bound to have put strain on ancient bands and clutches. You should drive with this potential hazard in mind.

These cars were essentially simple in mechanical specifications: The most uncommon overhaul will be of the electric window lifts. Air conditioning became an option in 1953, and cars so equipped should have their

Debutante showcar for 1950 GM Motorama used vast acreage of leopard-skin upholstery. Car would be quite a find today, but virtually all special GM Motorama cars have been destroyed ages ago. Note that Harley Earl began blending dashboard molding into forward upper corners of doors—a nice touch.

Coupe de Ville script appeared in rear quarter bright panel (C-pillar) on 1951 Coupe de Villes (but not on the 6237 "club coupe" hardtops). All 1951s had cross-hatched trim under headlamps, inboard parking lights. Dummy scoop at leading edge of rear fender was a Harley Earl touch that appeared in 1950.

Another view of the 331 ci overhead valve V-8. This is the 1953 version, with horsepower boosted to 210. It was long-lived and reliable; if found in good shape it may be counted on for generally trouble-free-service.

1949-53 Sixty-Two
ENGINE
Type: . . . . 8-cylinder 90° V-type, watercooled, cast iron block and heads
Bore x stroke: . . . . 3.81x3.63 in.
Displacement: . . . . 331.0 ci
Valve operation: . . . . overhead, pushrod actuated
Compression ratio: 1945-53: 7.51; 1953: 8.25:1
Carburetion: . . . . 1949-51: Carter dual downdraft; 1952-53: Carter two-stage four-barrel
Bhp: . . . . 1949-51: 160 bhp gross (133 net) at 3800 rpm; 1952: 190 bhp gross at 4000 rpm; 1953: 210 bhp gross at 4150 rpm
CHASSIS AND DRIVETRAIN
Transmission::3-spd. standard 1949. Hydra-matic optional 1949, standard 1950-on. Many '53s had Dynaflow because Hydra-matic shortage.
Rear axle ratio: . . . . 3.77:1; with Hydra-matic, 3.36:1, 3.70:1 optional through 1952; in 1953: 3.77:1
Rear suspension: . . . . . . live axle, semi-elliptic springs, tube shocks
Front suspension: . . . . independent, coil springs, tube shocks
GENERAL
Wheelbase: . . . . 126.0 in.
Overall length: . . . . sedans: 215.5 in.; other models in 1952-53: 220.5 in.
Track: . . . . 59 in. front, 63 in. rear
Tire size: 1949: 8.20x15; 1950-53: 8.00x15
Weight: . . . . 3863-4500 lb.
PERFORMANCE
As per Chapter 8

Another Motorama showcar used the smoother 1952 body but had major modifications. Panoramic windshield and flush-fit convertible top cover pre-figured the upcoming Eldorado; rear fender scoop was shorter than on production cars, twin antennas were different.

Cadillac became more glitzy than ever in 1953, as wire wheels began to be seen and enormous bumper guards were fitted (some with spring-loaded inset bullets—an early form of crash pro-tection). This Sixty-two convertible represents the epitome of Fifties motoring for people who had "made it." Peaked headlamp covers were another new feature for the successful 1953 model year.

Coupe de Ville availability on the collector market increases as you move through the fifties. Cadillac built about 10,000 more hardtops in 1953 than in 1950. For example, there were 14,550 of these Sixty-Twos, and they have survived in fairly decent quantity. Two-toned versions were more common than single colors; club expertise should be relied upon when repainting, to ensure authentic colors and combinations.

systems carefully checked by experts. Also pay attention to the brake system, which is required to put up with a considerable amount of power. Restorers have had success with silicon brake fluid, which does not allow water to accumulate in the lines and does no damage if spilled on paintwork.

The increasing amounts of plastic and brightwork that went into Cadillacs during the fifties must be considered as an added restoration headache. Take their condition into account when evaluating a purchase. Finally, these cars have displayed no significant increase in rust susceptibility—a check of all the common rust areas should suffice.

SUMMARY AND PROSPECTS

A check of the ratings assigned to various body styles and vintages will show that collectibility varies widely in this series of Sixty-Twos. The 1949 models were clearly the most timelessly styled, still as clean and handsome as the 1948 models despite a somewhat heavier grille. But the 1949 Cadillacs do not seem to hold any lead in value over the 1948s, despite their more modern engine. If anything, the old flathead is preferred; collectors are divided over the merits of the newer engine. The 1949 Sixty-Two coupe, convertible and Coupe de Ville are all rated as Milestones but, significantly, the rating stops there—cars from 1950 to 1953 don't rank with them. Beginning in 1950, Cadillacs got heavier and shinier, and by 1953 they were sporting what the British disdainfully called the "dollar grin." That chromey look hasn't appealed to American collectors either, and this should be borne in mind when considering a post-1949 Sixty-Two. Still, open models will out, and a 1953 Sixty-Two ragtop remains a highly desirable Cadillac.

PRODUCTION

	1949
Model 6207 club coupe	7,515
Model 6237 Coupe de Ville	2,150
Model 6267 convertible coupe	8,000
Model 6269 four-door sedan	37,977
Bare chassis	1

PRODUCTION

	1950	1951	1952	1953
Model 6219 four-door sedan	41,890	55,352	42,625	47,640
Model 6237 club coupe	6,434	10,132	10,065	14,353
Model 6237D Coupe de Ville	4,507	10,241	11,165	14,550
Model 6267 convertible coupe	6,986	6,117	6,400	8,367
Bare chassis	1	2	0	4

Sixty-Special
1949-53

HISTORY

During model year 1949, the Sixty-Special retained its 133-inch wheelbase and looked little different from its elegant 1948 predecessor, except for general restyling features such as the lower, slightly heavier grille. An experimental Coupe de Ville model was built, but alas there was only one. The four-door cars were more popular than ever, though, and Cadillac racked up 11,399 sales of the 1949.

By 1953 the Sixty-Special accounted for an even 20,000 units—a fine performance indeed for a car which by then cost a minimum of $4,305, and usually more like $5,000. Like other models, however, the Sixty-Special suffered aesthetically as the years passed; moreso from 1950 on because its wheelbase was reduced to 130 inches, only four inches longer than the standard Sixty-Two sedan. The ohv V-8 was installed in all these cars.

IDENTIFICATION

1949: Similar to 1948 with a more massive grille containing two instead of three rows of egg-crates.

1950: Stubbier looking thanks to a decrease in wheelbase. Rear quarter windows retained.

1951: Power window lifts became standard equipment.

The handsome, formal Sixty-Special for 1949, with a lower, somewhat heavier-looking grille. The identifying "scoop" in the rear fender and the four vertical bars on the roof quarters remained this year.

In common with smaller Cadillacs, the Sixty-Special was made heavier looking in 1950. It also lost its traditional "formal" rear roof quarter, and many feel a lot of distinction at the same time. To add insult to injury, the wheelbase was shortened three inches. Traditional vertical hashmarks were doubled in number as if to make up for all this, and applied low on forward part of rear fender.

The Sixty-Special for 1952 was more of the same, shown here with blackwalls, probably owing to Korean War shortages. Interiors were more colorful. In 1952, the Sixty-Special had light metallic leather and contrasting broadcloth. A plus for the model was its new 190 bhp engine and dual exhausts. Power steering, an option in 1952, is usually found on these models.

1952: Eight vertical chrome hashmarks on rear fenders directly behind the grille-type stoneguard.

1953: Few changes.

Hydra-matic transmission standard from 1950 on. Other styling changes same as for 1949-51 Sixty-One and 1949-53 Sixty-Two.

PERFORMANCE AND UTILITY

Remarks for 1949 are the same as those for 1949-53 Sixty-Two. The new V-8 was an important performance improvement in 1949, but in 1950 its advantage was obviated by a redesign which, though shorter in overall length, was no lighter. All that fancy trim hung on the Sixty-Special from 1950 on erased the 200 pounds shorn through the new V-8. For collectors, this renders the Milestone-rated 1949 model far more desirable than its immediate successors.

PROBLEM AREAS

See the 1948 and 1949-53 Sixty-Two.

SUMMARY AND PROSPECTS

For the 1949 model, reasonable prices prevail and investment potential is good. For the 1950-53 models, however, it is difficult to assign more than one star. While very well built and free of most long-term maladies, these cars have little distinction and stand relatively low in collector affections.

1949-53 Sixty-Special	
ENGINE	
As per Chapter 9	
CHASSIS AND DRIVETRAIN	
As per Chapter 9	
GENERAL	
Wheelbase:	1949: 133.0 in.; 1950-53: 130.0 in.
Overall length	1949: 226.0 in.; 1950-53: 224.5 in.
Track:	59 in. front, 63 in. rear
Tire size:	1949: 8.20x15; 1950-53: 8.00x15
Weight:	4129-4415 lb.
PERFORMANCE	
As per Chapter 8	

Brightwork increased along bottom of car and jumbo wheel covers added sparkle to Sixty-Specials in 1953. Horsepower went up to 210 and interiors received expanded color and fabric choices. Of all the post-1949 Sixty-Specials covered in this chapter, this is probably the most desirable.

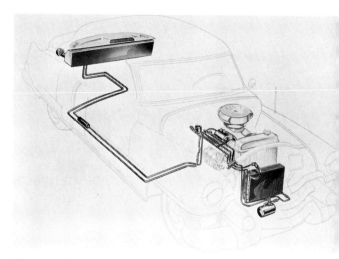

Air-conditioning components fill the package shelf of a 1953 Sixty-Special. This was its first year on Cadillacs since the abortive initial offering in 1941, though it was not often specified. Clear plastic ducts channeled stale air out of the car and through the system without obstructing rear view.

Diagram shows what to look for if you find an air-conditioned 1953 Cadillac—be sure it's all there. Big V-8 is perfectly capable of powering the compressor.

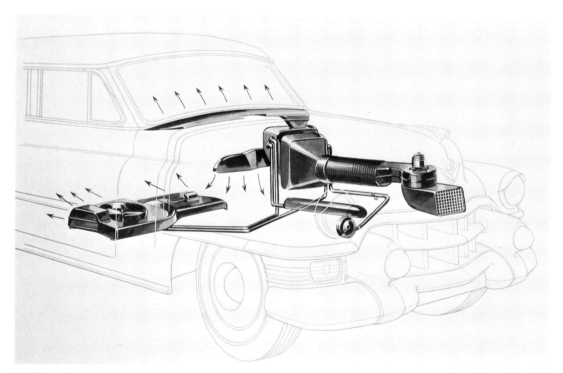

Cadillac also introduced a dual heating/ventilation system in 1953 which, unlike air, was standard. Oversize fan sucked in, heated, filtered and distrib- uted air to dash and front compartment; supplemental ducts and blower under front seat shot more heated air back to rear passengers.

1951 Sixty-Special.

Chapter 11

Seventy-Five
1950-53

★★★

HISTORY

The flagship of the fleet finally received the postwar body design starting in 1950: While the standard wheelbase grew from 136 to almost 147 inches, the commercial chassis wheelbase went from 163 to 157 inches. The Seventy-Fives of this period followed general styling directions of the junior Cadillacs, and duplicated their cheaper 1949-style dashboard. Cadillac had now rationalized the Seventy-Five down to two basic models: the seven-passenger sedan (no more five-passengers) and the imperial sedan with chauffeur partition. A handful of nine-passenger business sedans was built for export, while 2,000-3,000 commercial chassis were supplied each year to the hearse and ambulance custom coachbuilders.

IDENTIFICATION

Elongated versions of comparable 1950-53 Cadillacs, with fixed rear quarter windows aft of squared-up rear doors. Power windows became standard beginning in model year 1951 but Hydra-matic was still an option ($198 in 1953). Air conditioning available at $620 on the 1953 models. Rear window not extending around rear quarter.

PERFORMANCE AND UTILITY

Big, heavy, long cars which lack the old-age distinction of the Classic pre-1950

Much longer wheelbase added distinction to Seventy-Fives after the redesign in 1950. This is a styling rendering for the new body, originally to come out for 1949. Busy with the new V-8, Cadillac postponed the new Seventy-Five to 1950.

Seventy-Fives, these Cadillacs are considerably less important to collectors than their forebears. They are expensive to run (weighing over 5,000 pounds with two passengers aboard), and expensive to repair or restore, with more square yards of cloth, leather, carpeting and brightwork than anything else in the line. Like most long-wheelbase cars of the fifties, their collector appeal is limited, as is their ability to find happy homes as old cars.

PROBLEM AREAS

These big beasts are not beset with any extreme mechanical problems, though the Hydra-matic puts up with a lot in translating available power to the road, and should be carefully checked and maintained. The brakes, too, must be watched. The most severe problem, relative to other Cadillacs of the same vintage, is the money it takes to restore one. The very best example should be purchased regardless of price—it'll be cheaper in the long run. But it's easier to lay out more money for one of these than you'll soon get back.

SUMMARY AND PROSPECTS

Probably the least-desirable group considered thus far, though entirely up to par for what they were, the 1950-53 Seventy-Fives packed a lot of comfort and luxury into their big bodies. They are not too expensive to buy, relative to pre-1950 biggies, but they

1950-53 Seventy-Five
ENGINE
Type: .... 8-cylinder 90° V-type, watercooled, cast iron block and heads
Bore x stroke: .... 3.81x3.63 in.
Displacement: .... 331.0 ci
Valve operation: .... overhead, pushrod actuated
Compression ratio: 1950-52: 7.5:1; 1953: 8.25:1
Carburetion: ..... 1950-51: Carter dual downdraft; 1952-53: Carter two-stage four-barrel
Bhp: .... 1950-51: 160 bhp gross (133 net) at 3800 rpm; 1952: 190 bhp gross at 4000 rpm; 1953: 210 bhp gross at 4150 rpm
CHASSIS AND DRIVETRAIN
Transmission: ... 1950-52: 3-speed standard, Hydra-matic optional; 1953: Hydra-matic or Dynaflow standard
Rear axle ratio: .... manual: 4.27:1; automatic: 3.77:1
Rear suspension: ...... live axle, semi-elliptic springs, tube shocks
Front suspension: .... independent, coil springs, tube shocks
GENERAL
Wheelbase: .... 146.8 in.
Overall length: .... 236.5 in.
Track: .... 59 in. front, 63 in. rear
Tire size: 8.20x15
Weight: .... 4235-4850 lb.
PERFORMANCE
Acceleration: .... 0-60: 14 seconds
Top speed: .... 100 mph
Fuel mileage: .... 10-18 mpg

The 1951 Seventy-Five, showing typical 1951 face and otherwise unchanged 1950 limo body. Collectors should bear in mind that Seventy-Five side trim is not interchangeable with lesser models.

are also not inclined to rise rapidly in value. If you must have a limousine, this is the budget variety; it'll never be rated either a Classic or a Milestone.

PRODUCTION	1950	1951	1952	1953
Model 7523 sedan, 7-pass.	716	1,090	1,400	1,435
Model 7523L business sedan, 9-pass.	1	30	0	0
Model 7533 imperial, 7-pass.	743	1,085	800	765
Commercial chassis, 157 in. wheelbase	2,052	2,960	1,694	2,005

Compared to the previous picture this artist's rendering looks sensational but, typically for the time, it has been stretched to make the 1952 Seventy-Five appear longer and lower. Only styling details changed in 1952 were at front and rear.

The Fleetwood Seventy-Five for 1953, with detail styling following general theme of smaller models but not as chromey as Sixty-Specials.

Radiator Thermostat

Fuel Pump
Push Rod

Outlet Passage
for Crankcase Ventilation

Distributor and Oil Pump
Drive Gear

Rear Main
Bearing Oil Seal

Pilot Bearing

Harmonic Balancer

Timing Chain

Floating Oil Intake

Powering all 1952 Golden Anniversary Cadillacs was the 190 horsepower 331 V-8, fractionally smoother than earlier versions of the same engine, and livelier. Seventy-Fives needed all the life they could get.

Chapter 12

Eldorado
1953

★★★★★

HISTORY

Historically an important Cadillac, the Eldorado prefigured standard styling to come, which was quite rakish indeed. It featured the most powerful ohv V-8 yet offered: 210 bhp with 8.25:1 compression. Its advanced styling, shared with the Buick Skylark and Olds Fiesta, was—and is—its great contribution. There was a leather-cowled instrument panel, Cadillac's first production wraparound windshield, wire wheels, a lowered beltline and a fully disappearing top (it dropped into a metal-covered well behind the rear seat, creating a clean appear-ance). The top came in black or white Orlon; the body came in Aztec red, Azure blue, Alpine white or Artisan ochre; the interiors were color-keyed in full leather.

A swank, daring model with a host of new ideas to offer, the 1953 Eldo cost your up-and-coming film star or oil mogul a cool $7,750, and only a handful were sold. It has everything that excites the car collector juices today, though—and from the hobby standpoint it is the most important model Cadillac between 1950 and 1956. It is also the most expensive; you can only wish that $7,750 would buy a good one right now.

For 1953, wire wheels, otherwise optional at $325 that year, were part of the Eldo's equipment at $7,750. In equivalent currency, that would be $28,500 today.

IDENTIFICATION

Lower stance than Sixty-Two convertible, thanks to cut-down doors. Metal boot covers the lowered convertible top. No special Eldorado script or ornamentation, but windshield is unique. Front end styling otherwise follows 1953 regular line.

PERFORMANCE AND UTILITY

Some 300 pounds heavier than the stock convertible, the Eldorado is the slug of the line in performance, but it's only relative: With 210 gross bhp there's more than enough power for jack-rabbit starts and smooth cruising at any speed you care to travel, as long as it's in a straight line. Roadholding, which was so good in the 1949 Cadillacs, deteriorated as the cars added length and width and weight. It was no better or worse on the Eldorado than on any of the other 1953s, which means pretty awful. The Eldo was thirsty, too, as any 4,800 pound V-8 must be, but a regular blast for sunny-day cruisin'.

PROBLEM AREAS

If you can afford one (the best examples cost $25,000-30,000), you're probably braced for the possibility that if you prang a door panel or break the windshield, replacements are going to cost you (about $1,000 for the recent repro-windshield,). Low production resulted in few extra parts or trim bits. However, there's hardly anything that can't be made, given resourcefulness and bucks, so this problem may be relative. As to longevity, the Eldo is as good as its more standard counterparts, and not especially prone to rust.

SUMMARY AND PROSPECTS

Like all limited-production exotics, the 1953 Eldorado will continue to appreciate in

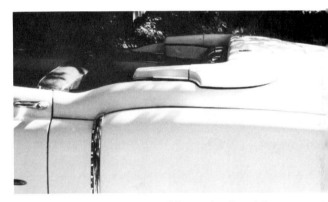

Eldorado soft top disappeared beneath all-metal boot, one of Harley Earl's notions. Boot flipped up from leading edge.

Clearly the most collectible Cadillac from 1946 through 1956, the 1953 Eldorado was a very limited super-convertible, Motorama-inspired with rakish cut-down beltline and flush-folding convertible top.

Switch to put top down might well have been confused with the left rear side window control, as they were identical. Upholstery was pleated leather.

1953 Eldorado

ENGINE

Type: . . . . 8-cylinder 90° V-type, watercooled, cast iron block and heads

Bore x stroke: . . . . 3.81x3.63 in.

Displacement: . . . . 331.0 ci

Valve operation: . . . . overhead, pushrod actuated

Compression ratio: 8.25:1

Carburetion: . . . . Carter two-stage four-barrel

Bhp: . . . . 210 bhp gross at 4150 rpm

CHASSIS AND DRIVETRAIN

Transmission: . . . . Hydra-matic

Rear axle ratio: 3.77:1

Rear suspension: . . . . . . live axle, semi-elliptic springs, tube shocks

Front suspension: . . . . independent, coil springs, tube shocks

GENERAL

Wheelbase: . . . . 126.0 in.

Overall length: . . . . 220.5 in.

Track: . . . . 59 in. front, 63 in. rear

Tire size: 8.00x15

Weight: . . . . 4800 lb.

PERFORMANCE

As per Chapter 8

value. The $25,000 you spend on one today —do buy the best one you can find—will probably increase at least as fast as the same amount sunk into a CD. The only Cadillac between the 1949 and the Eldorado Brougham with real individuality, it will remain largely a dream for most collectors; the fortunate few who own them will ever be envied.

PRODUCTION   *1953*
Model 6267S convertible coupe   532

Note: Officially part of the Sixty-Two series, the Eldorado was not broken out as a separate line until 1959, except for the limited Eldorado Brougham of 1957-58.

Appearing alongside new ''production'' Eldorado at GM Motorama was Cadillac's four-door hardtop showcar, the Orleans. Idea cars were never far from reality, and within three years Cadillac would have production four-door hardtops on the market. Instead or Orleans, they would be called Sedan de Villes. The whereabouts of the Orleans today is unknown, but a lot of people would like to know.

Four-barrel engine in this 1953 has a mean-looking air cleaner. (Cadillac La Salle Club, *Self-Starter Annual*)

Cadillac Goddess hood ornament is a smootheddown version of the classic ornament of the thirties. (Cadillac La Salle Club, *Self-Starter Annual*)

Bob Hoffmann's Eldorado shows off wraparound windshield, windwings, and beltline dip, all exclusive Eldorado features. (Cadillac La Salle Club, *Self-Starter Annual*)

Another view of Bob Hoffmann's car. (Cadillac La Salle Club *Self-Starter Annual*)

Dressy wire wheels can be seen on this 1953. (Cadillac La Salle Club, *Self-Starter Annual*)

Bob Hoffmann's Eldo in side view. (Cadillac La Salle Club, *Self-Starter Annual*)

Metal boot has a very nice fit and finish. (Cadillac La Salle Club, *Self-Starter Annual*)

Beltline dip of the Eldorados is accentuated by the graceful line of the rear fender. (Cadillac La Salle Club, *Self-Starter Annual*)

Fabulous closeup of Bob Hoffmann's 1953. (Cadillac La Salle Club, *Self-Starter Annual*)

Chapter 13

Sixty-Two
1954-56

★★★★ convertible
★★★ Coupe de Ville
★★ hardtop coupe
★★ Sedan de Ville (1956)
★ four-door sedan

HISTORY

A major restyle of the breadwinning Cadillac series, the 1954-56 generation featured longer, lower, wider, heavier cars with more power. The Sixty-Two's wheelbase was increased by three inches, and power from the 331 cid V-8 rose each year, from 230 to 250 and 285 bhp, respectively. Cadillac had a record year in 1955, selling 140,777 units. Yet in these three years the Sixty-Two was least changed annually than ever afterward.

The big, wide hood continued to tower over the front fenders; the deck was long, and set off by the traditional (but squarer) tailfin taillights. Wraparound windshields, introduced by Cadillac and others in 1953, were featured each year, along with a colorful variety of cloth, leather and vinyl upholstery and a wide choice of body paint colors, heavy on pastels.

These were the archetypal Cadillacs of the fifties, symbols of success-on-wheels. Dur-

Fully restyled 1954 Sixty-Two convertible can be told from 1955 model by round parking lights and gap between door molding and rear fender "scoop."

Wraparound windshield introduced on the 1953 Eldo was now applied to all Cadillac models.

ing this period the marque was never threatened in its preeminence by Lincoln, Packard or Imperial. A curious nomenclature change was "hardtop coupe" replacing the previous "coupe"—which was also a hardtop. The more luxurious Coupe de Ville remained a separate entity, priced about $400 higher. Sales of the base and CdV hardtops were approximately equal. A prototype Cadillac Sedan de Ville

was built in 1954, and produced as a regular model in 1956. Priced at $4,753, it enjoyed 41,732 sales for the model year, leading the Cadillac line in popularity.

IDENTIFICATION

Coupe de Ville identification carried in gold script above the rear fender.

1954: Two-toned tufted seats and door

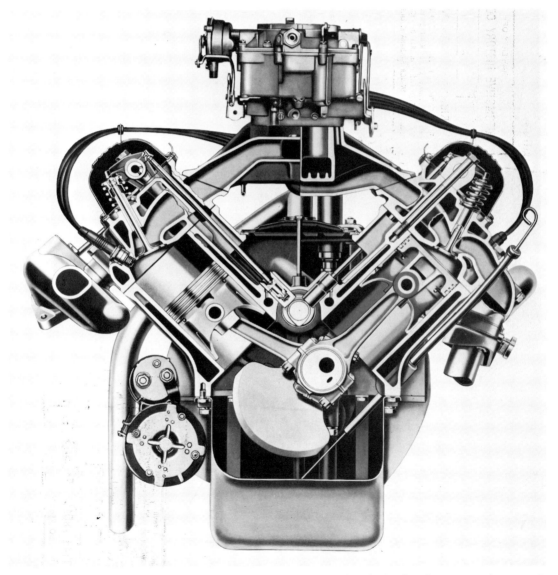

Horsepower went to 230 for the little-changed 1954 V-8 engine. The 1954-55 engines were reliable, but 1956 versions had soft rocker arms and were well-known troublemakers.

panels. One-piece panoramic windshield. Interior vent opening across full width of car under windshield base. Large, round parking lights set within the grille. Front fender/door molding does not meet rear vertical scoop. Dual circular exhaust pipes extend through bumper at rear.

1955: Parking lights now rectan- gular and located in front fenders under headlamps, outside grille. Six upright brightmetal bars on panel under deck lid above rear bumper. Simulated side scoop now extends only halfway down to join a chrome strip running the length of car. (Seventy-Five is slightly different.)

1956: Small mesh grille with Cadillac script across right half. Parking lights in oblong panels under bumper extensions. Rear fender bulge tapers back to raised exhaust extension outlet. Gold shield above side script.

PERFORMANCE AND UTILITY

These Cadillacs marked a trend toward greater bulk, poorer fuel mileage, higher running costs and higher performance. Whether the trade-offs appeal or not is a question only the individual can decide.

Many Cadillac collectors do have a marked preference for the crisper-styled 1954-56 generation over the 1950-53 models (the 1949 is well ahead of them both, however). These cars were fine over-the-road cruisers and did not necessarily require premium gas; they were the last Cadillacs through 1970 that didn't. The convertible model naturally retains the greatest appeal.

PROBLEM AREAS

The 1956 model was beset with mechanical problems and should be checked very carefully before purchase. Engines used soft rocker arms, and the characteristic "clickety-click" of 1956-58 V-8s is well-known among collectors. Rockers should be carefully maintained and checked frequently. Also in 1956, Cadillac introduced the first Slip-Away Hydra-matic, which offered smoother shifts but had many reliability problems that weren't cured until 1959.

Other problems are similar to those of the 1949-53 models. The increased amount of fancy trim makes restoration more costly than earlier models. The 1954-56 Cadillacs do not suffer much from rust, but door latches were part of a GM cost-cutting pro-

Sleeker in 1955, Sixty-Two was the same basic body as 1954, but stylists had cleverly integrated front/rear side styling. Horsepower was higher again. Parking lights were built into grille frame.

Convertibles are the most prized of this period, with the 1955 holding a very slight edge over the 1954, although the 1955 is more common in the field.

Cadillac Celebrity showcar graced 1955 Motoramas with wild new Sabre Spoke wheels, now a hot item in flea markets. This special also had a padded vinyl top and air conditioning. Sabres came standard on Eldorado, could be ordered on other models. Celebrity name showed up in production on a Chevy in 1982.

Most significant 1956 model was new four-door hardtop Sedan de Ville, easily the most popular model in the Sixty-Two line, selling upwards of 40,000 units. In general, 1956 Sixty-Twos had busier styling than the 1954-55 models. Engine and transmission problems beset all 1956s; any potential purchase should be considered carefully.

gram, and not as durable as earlier (or later) latches. Check these carefully and fix or replace.

SUMMARY AND PROSPECTS

The Sixty-Two convertibles are the most desirable cars of this generation. They have a sure lead over the Coupe de Ville, which is more commonplace due to increased production. The four-door hardtop Sedan de Ville for 1956 was an important new model for Cadillac, but has not appeared to move very fast with car collectors; it is assigned a two-star rating alongside the standard hardtop model. The four-door sedan, as usual, is the least likely to appreciate in future years due to its relatively mundane body styling and pillar construction. On the other hand, it stands to remain the tightest, quietest Sixty-Two of the lot for the very reason of its construction.

1954-56 Sixty-Two

ENGINE

Type: .... 8-cylinder 90° V-type, watercooled, cast iron block and heads
Bore x stroke: .... 1954-55: 3.81x3.63 in.; 1956: 4.00x3.63 in.
Displacement: .... 1954-55: 331.0 ci; 1956: 365.0 ci
Valve operation: .... overhead, pushrod actuated
Compression ratio: 1954: 8.25:1; 1955: 9.00:1; 1956: 9.75:1
Carburetion: .... Carter two-stage four-barrel
Bhp: ...... 1954: 230 bhp at 4400 rpm; 1955: 250 bhp at 4600 rpm; 1956: 285 bhp at 4600 rpm (all gross bhp)

CHASSIS AND DRIVETRAIN

Transmission: .... Hydra-matic
Rear axle ratio: .. 1954: 3.07:1, optional 3.36:1; 1955: 3.36:1, optional 3.07:1; 1956: 3.07:1, optional 3.36:1
Rear suspension: ...... live axle, semi-elliptic springs, tube shocks
Front suspension: .... independent, coil springs, tube shocks

GENERAL

Wheelbase: .... 129.0 in.
Overall length: .... 1954-55: sedans 216.4 in., others 223.4 in.; 1956: sedans 214.9 in., others 221.9 in.
Track: .... 60 in. front, 63 in. rear
Tire size: 1954: 8.20x15; 1955-56: 8.00x15
Weight: .... 4370-4625 lb.

PERFORMANCE

Acceleration: .... 0-80: 24 seconds
Top speed: .... 115 mph
Fuel mileage: .... 14 mpg at 70 mph

PRODUCTION	1954	1955	1956
Model 6219 four-door sedan	34,252	45,300	26,666
Model 6237 hardtop coupe	17,460	27,879	26,649
Model 6237D Coupe de Ville	17,170	33,300	24,086
Model 6239D Sedan de Ville	—	—	41,732
Model 6267 convertible coupe	6,310	8,150	8,300
Bare chassis	1	7	19

Chapter 14

Eldorado
1954-55

★★★★	convertible coupe
★★★	convertible coupe (1954, 1956)
★★★	Seville hardtop (1956)
	[all models Milestone]

HISTORY

Cadillac's prestige line remained part of the Sixty-Two series, but it underwent considerable revision during these years. Like the Buick Skylark, Eldorado in 1954 moved from a hyper-priced limited edition to a more affordable top-of-the-line model, losing some $3,000 in price via considerable homogenizing with off-the-shelf componentry. It was really nothing more than a gussied-up Sixty-Two convertible in 1954, with a broad, ribbed bright panel along the lower rear fender to distinguish it plus chrome wire wheels and a leather interior. In 1955 it departed from Sixty-Two styling and grew unique "shark-fin" rear fenders.

Production was up dramatically in both years, so in 1956 the fabulous Eldo branched off in two body styles: the convertible (now dubbed Biarritz) and a new hardtop coupe (called Seville—a name shared that year with a hardtop sedan DeSoto, but many years later resurrected on a revolutionary Cadillac). The Biarritz and Seville were, how-

There was a big change in Eldorado for 1954 (and another one for 1955). This version was a much less expensive, higher-volume model, and far less distinctive than the 1953, although it still had the char- acteristic metal top cover. In lieu of sharkfins, which were conjured up for 1955, designers gave 1954 a huge ribbed rear fender appliqué which encompassed the skirt. Production was 2,150.

ever, priced almost as high as the original Eldo of 1953, and did not sell particularly well, though combined they out-did previous Eldorados.

In 1954, Eldorado shared the standard 230 hp V-8, but in both 1955 and 1956 it had a high-performance version which was exclusively its own, boasting 15-20 bhp more than the standard engine. Interiors remained gloriously opulent and, in keeping with overall Cadillac trends, styling got louder each year, with more anodized gold in evidence by 1956. Big, heavy cars, the 1955-56 Eldorados had enough extra urge under the hood to more than make up for their gains in avoirdupois.

IDENTIFICATION

1954: A wide, brightmetal, ribbed lower rear fender appliqué including the fender skirt, surmounted by a gold Cadillac crest. Chrome wire wheels. Fiberglass convertible top cover. Full leather interior.

1955: Distinctive shark-fin rear-fender styling with taillamps and back-up lamps carried in dual cylinders below. Rear fender appliqué deleted and skirts dropped in favor of larger wheel openings. Sabre-Spoke wire wheels instead of previous chrome wires. Brightmetal trim along beltline. Eldorado script on deck.

1956: Same styling, but featured unique dual-blade hood mascot. Gold anodized grille and gold wheels were no-cost options.

PERFORMANCE AND UTILITY

The same comments apply as those of 1954-56 Sixty-Twos, with the inevitable addition of higher running costs in 1955-56 thanks to the higher-performance V-8 engine. These were a handful on any road smaller or twistier than an interstate highway.

PROBLEM AREAS

These were similar to those of the 1954-56 Sixty-Two, with the additional problem of high restoration costs for gold anodized trim. The Sabre-Spoke wheels of the 1955-56 are highly sought by collectors; a set of them in fine condition will cost four figures all by themselves. The Eldorado Seville roof was covered with Vicodec fabric with two longitudinal seams; restoration is not com-

Famous Eldo sharkfins came in 1955; likewise, rear fender scoop and front fender/door molding were joined as in less expensive models. Brightwork along beltline, introduced in 1954, was retained.

Cadillac doubled its Eldorado sales this year, and 1955s are more common on the collector market. Being more distinctive, they enjoy definite preference over 1954s among collectors.

plicated, but finding the correct replacement material, or a near copy, may be difficult.

SUMMARY AND PROSPECTS

The Milestone Car Society—almost moribund but still researching its well-known list of postwar greats—in 1984 named all Eldorados from 1954 through 1958 Milestones, correcting a previous inconsistency. (Before this decision, only the 1953, 1955 and 1967 Eldorados, and 1957-58 Eldo Broughams, were listed.) This was a considerable boost to the collectibility of the 1954 and 1956 models, but the 1955 Eldorado thus far retains a slight lead in collector preference and appreciation. Both the 1954 and 1956 convertibles are less cleanly styled, and the 1955 is distinctive. The Seville hardtop was the more popular Eldo of 1956, but it has not risen in value as quickly as the ragtop 1955.

PRODUCTION	1954	1955	1956
Model 6267S convertible coupe*	2,150	3,950	2,150
Model 6237S Seville hardtop coupe	—	—	3,900

*Biarritz in 1956.

1954-56 Eldorado
ENGINE
Type: . . . . 8-cylinder 90° V-type, watercooled, cast iron block and heads
Bore x stroke: . . . . 1954-55:3.81x3.63 in.; 1956: 4.00x3.63 in.
Displacement: . . . . 1954-55: 331.0 ci; 1956: 365.0 ci
Valve operation: . . . . overhead, pushrod actuated
Compression ratio: 1954: 8.25:1; 1955: 9.00:1; 1956: 9.75:1
Carburetion: . . . . 1954: Carter or Rochester 4bbl; 1955-56: two Carter 4bbl
Bhp: . . . . . . 1954: 230 bhp at 4400 rpm; 1955: 270 bhp at 4600 rpm; 1956: 305 bhp at 4700 rpm (all gross bhp)
CHASSIS AND DRIVETRAIN
As per Chapter 13
GENERAL
Wheelbase: . . . . 129.0 in.
Overall length: . . . . 1954-55: 223.4 in.; 1956: 221.9 in.
Track: . . . . 60 in. front, 63 in. rear
Tire size: 8.20x15
Weight: . . . . 4665-4880 lb.
PERFORMANCE
Acceleration: . . . . 0-80: 22 seconds
Top speed: . . . . 118 mph
Fuel mileage: . . . . 12 mpg at 70 mph

Another 1955 Eldorado. All 1955 Cadillacs carried six vertical brightmetal bars on lower deck under trunk lid. Identifying tailfinned 1955 Eldo is easy, but these bars serve to tell any 1955 at a glance, as well.

Eldorado made its first profit in 1955, so in 1956 it was split into hardtop Seville and convertible Biarritz models. Horsepower became 305. Sabre Spokes and full rear wheel cutouts were held over from 1955. The 1956 convertible is a scarce Eldo; it was outsold two to one by the Seville hardtop. Nevertheless, in view of engine and transmission problems that year, I would prefer a 1954 to a 1956.

Chapter 15

Sixty-Special
1954-56

★★

HISTORY

Following the 1954 design game plan, when the Sixty-Two moved up to a 129-inch wheelbase, the Sixty-Special went to 133 inches. Like the junior line it gained weight, and expanded in size in every direction. Its main appeal lay in its clear expression of what the owner thought of himself or herself, or would like everyone else to think of them also. A deck that stuck out a country mile beyond a conventional Sixty-Two was probably a plus at the country club, even though the rest of the car was physically little different from the smaller sedan. Per-

The 1954 Sixty-Special went back to its 133-inch wheelbase and looked more dignified as a result, but styling was a recognizable evolution from previous 1950s models. Like Seventy-Fives, body trim for these cars is hard to find, despite the fact that Cadillac built 16,000-18,000 per year.

haps the public saw this as a negative factor, for sales in this period were never as high as in 1953.

IDENTIFICATION

Eight vertical, chrome dummy louvers on the rear doors just aft of the dummy scoop, and an obviously longer-than-usual deck bearing Fleetwood script.

1955: Louvers moved to the extreme ends of the rear fenders (twelve of them on each side). Wide brightmolding covered lower portions of rear fenders and standard (small) skirt.

1956: New bulging moldings of the Cadillac rear fenders were capped in chrome on Sixty-Specials. Grille could be ordered in anodized gold like the Eldorado.

PERFORMANCE AND UTILITY

Similar to that of the 1954-56 Sixty-Two. However, the addition of even greater weight resulted in lower performance, since the Sixty-Special did not benefit from a high-performance engine as did the 1955-56 Eldorado. The Sixty-Special's four-inch-greater wheelbase seemed to add little to interior room while adding a great deal of bulk to the exterior, perhaps because of the extra trunk area which hung out in the rear. This was a much bulkier car than the Sixty-Two: In 1953 it had been only nine inches longer, now it was thirteen inches longer, the difference being entirely in the trunk area. (The models retained their four-inch-wheelbase difference.)

Here's the secret to the Sixty-Special's success—a big deck that stuck out much farther than your conventional Caddy or Packard, and the magic Fleetwood name on the trunk lid. This is a 1954 model.

Hardly any changes occurred in Sixty-Special styling for 1955 except those applied throughout the line—but identifying hashmarks moved back to the end of the rear fender. Collectors are divided on the merits of 1954 versus 1955 models; both are more popular than the 1956.

PROBLEM AREAS

It shared the problems of the 1954-56 Sixty-Special and 1954-56 Eldorado, with the addition of scarce body trim parts common only to Sixty-Specials. Prospective buyers should ensure that all the trim is there and in good shape—or at least restorable.

SUMMARY AND PROSPECTS

Relative to other Cadillacs, there's little to recommend these cars except their size and their admitted luxury—and the name Fleetwood, which still means much to some people. No post-1949 Sixty-Special has been named a Milestone car—with good reason.

PRODUCTION	1954	1955	1956
Model 6019			
four-door sedan	16,200	18,300	17,000

Sixty-Special for 1956 lost more distinction. Hashmarks migrated to tapered rear fender pods, which were capped in bright moldings. The name appeared in script on the fender. It was almost as if they were trying too hard to tell us what it was. No Sixty-Specials from this period are highly collectible; they are unlikely to become so.

Chapter 16

Seventy-Five
1954-67

★★ (1954-65)
★★★ (1965-67)

HISTORY

Along with the junior models, the "professional" Cadillac jumped three inches in wheelbase in 1954—but there it remained through 1970. Its bodywork was among the least changed in American cars of this period. What did change over the years were the front and rear ends, which varied with styling shuffles through 1960 and beyond. This was the year of the huge dogleg A-pillar and wraparound windshield, a styling fillip that aged rapidly but was still present on Seventy-Fives through 1965. In 1966, the Seventy-Five suddenly became contemporary again— smooth and finless, much more formal and elegant. A number were built with the $2,000 Landau roof option, which cluttered things up again but gave a lot of privacy with its small rear window and closed rear roof quarters.

Largely for commercial and professional use, Seventy-Fives typically came as huge nine-passenger sedans or as limousines with a division window—but many more bare chassis were produced for hearse, ambulance and specialty bodybuilders. This was the quintessential funeral carriage in a time when all former rivals, or almost all, had largely quit the field.

IDENTIFICATION

General styling as for junior models

Essential body of the 1954 Seventy-Five would be retained for 17 years, although below-beltline styling changes were many and varied in this period. The original 1954 is arguably one of the nicest.

through all years at front and rear. Though facelifts occurred from 1956 through 1959, the 1959 passenger "cage" and inner sheet metal were left alone through 1965 and only minor styling alterations were made at the ends. All-new body in 1966 matched contemporary junior models. The 1967 version was little changed but can be identified by its unbisected grille.

PERFORMANCE AND UTILITY

These things weighed about 2½ tons, were powered by nothing more than the base Cadillac engines, and were none too easy to drive, park or store. They were tremendous road cars, though, and blessed with a silky silence and floating ride that far exceeded even the high levels of the smaller Cadillacs. They were very thirsty and ex-

Unlike other 1955s, Seventy-Five side trim was not connected—car was simply too long. Moldings were therefore 1954 carryovers. Front end received rectangular 1955 parking lamps.

The 1956 Seventy-Five was less garish looking than the Sixty-Special, probably because the Seventy-Five owner didn't have to impress anybody.

pensive to maintain—not a car for everyone, even in the collector community.

PROBLEM AREAS

It may be difficult to replace exclusive components, although some outer body panels and hardware interchange with junior models of the same year. These cars are electrically complicated and very expensive to restore, due to the sheer volume of quality materials involved, if nothing else. They are best purchased after limited use by careful owners.

Rust is an increasing problem in examples built after 1956, particularly those in the sixties. There were few driveability problems through 1967 (the last year before federal emission controls), but these increased year by year from 1968.

SUMMARY AND PROSPECTS

One finds it hard to recommend a Cadillac Seventy-Five as a collector car, but for sheer presence and awesome size it can't be beat.

They are relatively rare, though rarity is not much of a factor here. Whether you really need one of these behemoths is a question you must ponder closely. Depreciation is

---

1954-67 Seventy-Five
ENGINE
As per model Sixty-Two for the same years
CHASSIS AND DRIVETRAIN
Transmission: . . . . Hydra-matic
Rear axle ratio: . . . . 1954-55: 3.77:1; 1956-57: 3.36:1; 1958: 3.07:1, optional 3.77:1; 1959-67: 3.36:1, optional 3.77:1, 3.21:1 with air
Rear suspension: . . . . . . live axle, semi-elliptic springs, tube shocks; 1957: coil springs
Front suspension: . . . . independent, coil springs, tube shocks
Frame: . . . . 1954-56: ladder type; 1957-65: backbone type; 1966-67: full perimeter
GENERAL
Wheelbase: . . . . 149.8 in.
Overall length: . . . . 237.3-244.5 in.
Track: . . . . 62.5-63.0 in. front and rear
Tire size: 8.20x15
Weight: . . . . 5055-5436 lb.
PERFORMANCE
Acceleration: . . . . 0-60: 15-18 seconds
Top speed: . . . . 110-115 mph
Fuel mileage: . . . . 10-16 mpg

Severe dog-leg wrapped windshield and doors cut into the roof were new features on the Seventy-Five limousine in 1957.

severe: In 1982 a 1976 limo that sold new for $16,000 was worth $5,000. On the other hand, the depreciation makes it pretty cheap per pound!

PRODUCTION

	1954	1955	1956	1957	1958
Model 7523 8-pass. sedan*	889	1,075	1,095	1,010	802
Model 7533 8-pass. limo*	611	841	955	890	730
Bare chassis, 156/158 in. wheelbase	1,635	1,975	2,025	2,169	1,915

* 9-pass. in 1958.

	1959	1960	1961	1962	1963
Model 6723 9-pass. sedan	710	718	600	696	680
Model 6733 9-pass. limo	690	832	926	904	795
Bare chassis, 156 in. wheelbase	2,102	2,160	2,204	2,280	2,527

	1964	1965	1966	1967
Model 6723/69723 9-pass. sedan	617	455	980	835
Model 6733/69733 9-pass. limo	808	795	1,037	965
Bare chassis, 156 in. wheelbase	2,639	2,669	2,463	2,333

NOTES ON LATER MODELS

From 1968, Seventy-Fives received the new, larger 472 V-8 with 375 gross hp, while dimensions remained unchanged at 149.8 inches for the wheelbase and twenty feet four inches overall length. A complete re-style occurred for 1971, when the cars gained an inch and a fraction in wheelbase and sleek, more rounded styling reminiscent of the contemporary Sixty-Specials. For several years, doors extended into the roof for ease of exit and entry. From 1970 there were dual-level air conditioning and climate control. Also in 1971, the commercial chassis

Sophistication was lost, many think, when the Seventy-Five went to Eldo-type sharkfins in 1958. Chromey 1958 grille was equally unbecoming.

was lengthened 1½ inches, to 157½ inches.

Cadillac continued to produce about 2,000 commercial Seventy-Five chassis for hearse, ambulance and florist delivery car manufacturers; these were by then the only long-wheelbase formal cars built as limousines in North America. Armbruster/Stageway of Arkansas found the impressive length not quite enough, and built a twenty-two-foot-long Silverhawk Executive Limousine out of a Fleetwood Brougham, which rivaled the production Seventy-Fives.

But the age of downsizing was to come, even in this rarified atmosphere. In 1977 (one year after the revolutionary Seville), Cadillac dropped its biggest wheelbase to 144½ inches. Another tradition fell that year when the Seventy-Five designation passed into history. The cars were known only as Fleetwoods in 1977, and have been referred

The Seventy-Five survived the Year of the Fin remarkably well; it was really too long to be overbalanced by the tailfins that looked so huge and out of place on standard-sized Cadillacs.

Fins were vanishing in a hurry by 1960 but the huge compound-curved windshield was still there. This is not something today's Cadillac enthusiast wants to have to replace.

Fins were only vestigial by 1965; Fleetwood limousine shown here has landau roof treatment, which allows certain privacy in the back.

In 1966 the Seventy-Five long sedan and limousine were completely restyled, receiving the first major body change since 1959. Look for standard auto-matic heating and air-conditioning dual system for front and rear on these cars; automatic load leveler had been introduced on the 1965 models.

to as Fleetwood Limousines since 1978.

The basic road-ready Cadillac offerings in this field have, to date, been a nine-passenger sedan and a formal sedan. Remarkably, their base prices didn't exceed $30,000 until 1983, and today they are probably the best bargains in the executive car class—whether or not this is a plus or a minus we should not, perhaps, speculate.

Considerable technical complexity attends all Fleetwood Seventy-Fives of recent years; in this writer's day a kid was expected to be able to take an M.G. TC completely apart and put it back together again, restored, with little more than a shop manual. Not even genius kids would attempt that with a Fleetwood Seventy-Five limousine.

These Cadillacs may be summarized as follows: enormous in every dimension (though not as big now as they were in the seventies); expensive to buy, run and live with; impossible to restore; absolute bears to service; of little collector potential; and about the most impressive things still rolling out of the guarded citadels of General Motors.

The 1967 Seventy-Five was only slightly restyled; this is the limousine model.

80

Chapter 17

Sixty-Two
1957-58

★★★★	convertible
★★★	Coupe de Ville
★★	hardtop coupe
★★	Sedan de Ville
★	hardtop sedan

HISTORY

Years of radical change for Cadillac saw all-new styling in 1957, along with a tubular-center X-type chassis-frame which cut weight by a dramatic 475 pounds. That year also offered an opportunity to do away with the four-door sedan, which almost seemed to be headed for extinction in those days.

Cadillac substituted a four-door hardtop, detrimmed somewhat from the more posh Sedan de Ville.

One trouble with the handsome 1957 line was that there were too many models ending in "ille," and the Sixty-Two range was itself getting crowded. (Cadillac was one of the first to acknowledge that, and model

Distinctive and elegant in an age of ostentation, the 1957 Cadillac tailfin wasn't outlandish enough to satisfy everyone. I'd take a 1957 any day compared to a 1958. Little collector movement has occurred with either.

rationalization arrived in 1959.) Unfortunately, the good-looking 1957 models were superseded by the gaudy 1958s, which helped Cadillac and its brothers celebrate GM's fiftieth anniversary with an astounding crash. The Recession had something to do with it, but production was down across the board and it was a dreadful year.

The 1958 really reaped what it deserved. The only reason I haven't downgraded its star rating is because I recognize some people love the things. Say what you want, a grille full of chrome studs, shark fins borrowed from the Eldorado, massive chrome and brushed stainless everywhere, and a swaybacked body shape were as good a testimony as ever to the old European taunt that the United States is the only country to have progressed from barbarism to decadence without an intervening period of civilization.

IDENTIFICATION

1957: Small, trapezoid-shaped fine-mesh grille guarded by large canted bumpers with rubber-tipped ends, two parking lights on either side. Small dummy scoops under the shrouded headlamps. No brightwork on front

It's not easy to tell this Sixty-Two hardtop from the high-line Coupe de Ville, but you ought to know; this one has Cadillac instead of Coupe de Ville script on front fender. Interior trim is more modest. Collectors favor the Coupe de Ville.

Traditional best bet among body styles, Sixty-Two convertible was particularly nice in 1957. This is one of the most affordable luxury convertibles of the fifties with any claim to decent styling.

fenders. Last year for single headlamps. Clean, modest, square-ended tailfins. Black-tipped bumper guards. Mesh grilles.

1958: First year for quad headlamps (except Eldorado Brougham). Dirty, outlandish, pointed tailfins. Black-tipped bumper guards. Full-width grilles with straight (not canted)

bumpers/guards, filled with square baubles that look like a thousand rejected cuff links. Oblong parking lights. Chrome on front fenders tapering back from headlamp housing. Chrome on rear fenders.

PERFORMANCE AND UTILITY

Cadillac enlarged its V-8 for the first time in 1956, to 365 cubic inches. In 1957 this engine developed 300 gross hp, and 310 in 1958. This provided more than ample power but, since no Sixty-Two weighed less than 4,500 pounds, these cars can hardly be called rockets. High-speed cruising was good, so as open-road cars they excel. Expensive to operate and fuel, 1957-58 Cadillacs remain well built, solid and not too susceptible to rust, which really reared its ugly head the following year. (This was fairly unique for 1957-58, when rust became an almost industrywide epidemic in Detroit.)

PROBLEM AREAS

The soft rocker arms on all 1957-58 V-8s lead to rocker noise and eventual failure as they did for 1954-56 Sixty-Twos. This problem wasn't cured until the 390 came in for 1959. The Slip-Away Hydra-matic, intro-

Two major headaches for 1957 owners were the soft-rocker engine (now 365 cid, 300 hp, 10:1 compression) and the Hydra-matic transmission. Neither problem was entirely worked out until 1959.

Sedan de Ville was 1957's most desirable four-door Cadillac, but there weren't many takers.

1957-58 Sixty-Two

ENGINE

Type: . . . . 8-cylinder 90° V-type, watercooled, cast iron block and heads
Bore x stroke: . . . . 4.00x3.63 in.
Displacement: . . . . 365.0 ci
Valve operation: . . . . overhead, pushrod actuated
Compression ratio: 1957: 10.0:1; 1958: 10.25:1
Carburetion: . . . . 1957: Rochester #7015701 4bbl; 1958: Carter #2862S 4bbl
Bhp: . . . . . . 1957: 300 bhp at 4800 rpm; 1958: 310 bhp at 4800 rpm (gross)

CHASSIS AND DRIVETRAIN

Transmission: . . . . Hydra-matic
Rear axle ratio: . . . . 3.07:1 (other ratios available)
Rear suspension: . . . . live axle, helical coil springs, tube shocks
Front suspension: . . . . independent, coil springs, tube shocks
Air suspension: . . . . optional 1958: central compressor and accumulator, self leveling, with four-link rear suspension and air bags or coil springs
Frame: . . . . first year for tubular X-frame without side rails

GENERAL

Wheelbase: . . . . 129.5 in.
Overall length: . . . . 1957: 220.9 in.; 1958: 221.8 in.
Track: . . . . 61 in. front and rear
Tire size: 8.20x15
Weight: . . . . 4677-4856 lb.

PERFORMANCE

Acceleration: . . . . 0-60: 12 seconds
Top speed: . . . . 115 mph
Fuel mileage: . . . . 12-18 mpg

duced the year before, continued to give reliability problems on the 1957 models, but was improved in 1958. If Hydros worry you, look for a 1958 model, not a 1957.

Interior and exterior trim parts are in short supply. Generally high running costs can be assumed. Rust is not of epidemic proportions. In 1958, air suspension was optional and should be viewed as a serious problem area, expensive to fix.

SUMMARY AND PROSPECTS

These are minor-league entries among Cadillac collectibles, but triple-A members of that league. The 1957s were fresh and original looking, though their lines haven't worn too well. The 1958s were garish and decadent, making up for what they lost in looks by more reliable mechanicals. Aesthetically a question mark, but clean examples will continue to appreciate modestly, and sportier body styles are good investments.

The least expensive 1958 Cadillac was the Sixty-Two hardtop at $4,694. It is also one of the least collectible of a little-collected year.

PRODUCTION	1957	1958
Model 6237		
hardtop coupe	25,120	18,736
Model 6237D		
Coupe de Ville	23,813	18,414
Model 6239		
hardtop sedan	32,342	13,335
Model 6239D		
Sedan de Ville	23,808	23,989
Model 6239E		
hardtop sedan (extra deck)	—	20,952
Model 6267		
convertible coupe	9,000	7,825
Bare chassis and export	385	206

Sixty-two convertible for 1958 had all the glitz thought possible, although a bit more was found for the Sixty-Special. It is the most desirable 1958 next to Eldorado, but that's not saying much.

A new variation was the extended-deck sedan option in the Sixty-Two range for 1958. It was 8½ inches longer than the normal model and cost $188 more. Over 20,000 were built, making the normal Sixty-Two hardtop sedan much scarcer.

Eldorado
1957-58

★★★★	**Biarritz**
★★★	**Seville**
	[all models Milestone]

HISTORY

The two models of Eldorado continued in 1957 and 1958, still within the Sixty-Two series. They carried the usual round of exclusive features and special styling deviations, most prominent of which were large shark-fins growing out of the rounded stern —distinctive from the 1957 design. In both years the Eldorados wore largely conventional Cadillac front ends, although they did not carry hood ornaments. In addition to the two-door models, Cadillac records the production of four model 6239S Seville hardtop sedans, nominally priced at the same $7,286 that bought a convertible or hardtop coupe. The 1957 Eldorados continued to offer a specially tuned (325 hp) version of the 365 V-8, while the 1958 models had triple Rochester two-barrels and 355 bhp.

IDENTIFICATION

Stock Cadillac up front except for lack of

Eldorado Biarritz convertible for 1957. Retained in new body style were Eldo's sharkfin taillamps and Sabre Spoke wheels. Certified as a Milestone, this and its 1958 successor were the last really distinctively styled Eldos. Highly collectible.

hood ornaments. Rear ends rounded downward with round taillamps and large, thin-section, pointed tailfins. Open rear wheel openings swathed in brightmetal trim.

1958: Ten vertical chrome dummy louvers ahead of rear wheel arches (similar to 1942-56 Sixty-Special trim). Narrow V on lower-left corner of rear deck lids. Name in block letters next to V.

PERFORMANCE AND UTILITY

The 1957 version, with the hottest V-8 yet offered in a Cadillac, was a top-of-the-line performer. It could move out with the best of the 1957 competition, despite its nearly 5,000 pounds of curb weight. Performance was somewhat peppier with the 1958 tri-carb setup, which delivered an impressive 355 bhp. Big cars that handled fairly well for their size, though by no means gymkhana equipment, Eldos were at their best on the open highway. They were expensive to operate, as always, and very thirsty. Optional air suspension for 1958 gave some ride/handling improvement at the expense of reliability.

The 1958 Biarritz was similar to the 1957 at the rear but carried 1958-standard quad lamps and multiglitter grille up front, plus hashmarks on rear fender. The 1957 is a somewhat better investment.

Seville hardtop version of Eldorado for 1958; Sevilles are not nearly as desirable as Eldos, but command premium prices compared to other Cadillacs.

PROBLEM AREAS

The usual problems of replacing parts exist for these cars, especially in areas where they are unique: interior trim and exterior hardware. General drivetrain parts are less of a problem. It shared the problems of the optional 1958 air suspension with the Brougham. The oversquare, bored-out 365 V-8 was a solid, reliable engine, not known for its economy but able to lead a strong life even with six-figure mileage. These cars have greater rust susceptibility than standard Sixty-Twos. Costs of restoration are relatively high.

SUMMARY AND PROSPECTS

The last really specially styled Eldorados for some time, all versions of this group now are recognized as Milestone cars, which should enhance their collectibility in the future. As Eldorados go, they are not formidably priced, though definitely a lot more expensive than Sixty-Twos of comparable body styles. Finding one of the four hardtop sedans would be a coup for a collector; as always, the open car retains a decisive lead over the hardtop in value and appreciation potential. Their styling isn't ageless, but these were undoubtedly products of their time. With that in mind, some of the design excesses should be forgiven. Very low production lends desirability.

PRODUCTION

	1957	1958
Model 6237S		
Seville hardtop coupe	2,100	855
Model 6239S		
Seville hardtop sedan	4	—
Model 6267S		
Biarritz convertible	1,800	815

1957-58 Eldorado

ENGINE
Type: . . . . 8-cylinder 90° V-type, watercooled, cast iron block and heads
Bore x stroke: . . . . 4.00x3.63 in.
Displacement: . . . . 365.0 ci
Valve operation: . . . . overhead, pushrod actuated
Compression ratio: 1957: 10.0:1; 1958: 10.25:1
Carburetor:...1957: two Carter #2584S/2583S 4bbl; 1958: three Rochester #7015801 2bbl
Bhp:1957: 325 bhp at 4800 rpm; 355 bhp at 4800 rpm (gross)
CHASSIS AND DRIVETRAIN
As per Chapter 17
GENERAL
Wheelbase: . . . . 129.5 in.
Overall length: . . . . 220.9 in.; 1958: 221.8 in.
Track: . . . . 61 in. front and rear
Tire size: 8.20x15
Weight: . . . . 4810-4930 lb.
PERFORMANCE
As per Chapter 17

Chapter 19

Eldorado Brougham
1957-58

$$\boxed{\bigstar\bigstar\bigstar\bigstar\bigstar \text{ [Milestone]}}$$

HISTORY

Today the most desirable late Cadillac in collector circles, the Eldo Brougham was one of the first cars to gain Milestone status, and for lots of good reasons. Priced at a towering $13,074, it was billed as the last word in automotive sophistication, but saw fewer than 1,000 copies through both model years. Prices paid for fine examples lately have been monumental.

The Brougham was Cadillac's answer to the Continental Mark II and, like the Mark, it lost money on every sale. Derived from Motorama showcars like the pillarless four-door 1953 Orleans and the 1954 Park Avenue, it was a pillarless sedan of superlative finish, immediately recognizable with its brushed aluminum roof. A "wündercar" boasting every conceivable gadget, it was flashy where the Mark II was understated, exotic where the Mark II was conventional. All the usual power options were featured—plus electric door locks and trunk lid; a dual heating system; and a glovebox packed with

Non-running fiberglass showcar was reconfigured several times. Production Broughams had chrome rocker panel moldings and forged aluminum and steel fluted wheels, not "Sabre-Spoke" wheels as here.

Fiberglass prototype with thin metal strip between bumper and fender skirt, not used in production. Traditional Eldorado sharkfins were used, but much Brougham hardware is unique and hard to find.

magnetized silver tumblers, cigarette and tissue dispensers, lipstick and Arpege cologne in a special atomizer. There were forty-five choices of interior color and trim, including Karakul or lambskin carpeting.

But chief among the Brougham's special characteristics was its unique air suspension —four rubber domes replacing conventional springs at each wheel. The air chambers were fed by a small compressor integral with the power steering unit. Three levelers kept constant body height regardless or road or load. The system was a hastily designed reply to Packard's Torsion-level novelty of 1955. It was not reliable in practice, but it did give Cadillac something to talk about.

In retrospect, the Cadillac Eldorado Brougham of 1957-58 was a striking example of overengineering and underdevelopment. But despite its faults, it was a fabulous automobile, and deserves every bit of the interest and enthusiasm that surround it

The 1958 Eldorado Brougham had no exterior differences from the 1957, but three two-barrel Rochesters and leather trimmed interior door panels (metal in 1957) are points of identification.

today. Since the 1949 models with the revolutionary new V-8, there had not been such a total break with Cadillac's past. Although it was a failure as a product, the Brougham did inspire a new upper-class, limited-edition marketing approach. It also gave the Eldorado name a reputation for engineering advances as well as unique styling. This reputation continued in the sixties, when Cadillac produced the first of its front-wheel-drive cars under the Eldorado nameplate.

IDENTIFICATION

Only Cadillac with quad headlights in 1957 (and the only 1957 with them except for Nash). Brushed stainless steel roof was a unique feature of both 1957 and 1958 models. Clean lines, with pointed shark-fin rear fenders. The 1957 style of grillework was retained in 1958, while other Cadillacs moved into the jukebox business. Only two things distinguish a 1957 from a 1958 model: (1) the

Glitzy cockpit of fiberglass prototype is generally stock, but rearview mirror was hung from top of windshield on the production versions.

A 1958 Eldorado Brougham belonging to a California enthusiast, in the very handsome silver paint job, which blends beautifully with brushed stainless roof.

Narrow-band whitewalls were correct on 1957-58 Broughams. (Bud Juneau)

1947 had metal interior door panels painted to match interior color, while 1958 panels were leather upholstered; (2) the 1957 had two four-barrel carburetors, while the 1958 had tri-carbs.

PERFORMANCE AND UTILITY

The Brougham looked and felt more compact than other 1957-58 models, although its wheelbase was only a half-inch shorter than the Sixty-Two's. It had astonishingly good handling characteristics for a Cadillac of the fifties. Its air-sprung ride was very smooth and silky, even by Cadillac standards—evidence of the extra care that went into its assembly. This car came wonderfully equipped with every possible power gadget, but it was very thirsty.

The Brougham was not as rapid as a standard Eldorado in 1957. Despite its 325 hp engine, it weighed about 400 pounds more than a Biarritz or Seville. In 1958, the Brougham shared the normal 310 hp engine with the rest of the line, and was consequently even slower than in 1957.

PROBLEM AREAS

Most Eldorado Broughams have had their air domes replaced. The lack of adequate research and development almost guaranteed that the domes would blow or spring leaks in the field. They did so with abandon, causing many a Brougham to sink down on its haunches overnight, acting like a Citroën with terminal hydraulic thirst. Contemporary owners converted to conventional coil springs at their local dealerships for about $400 a crack, but this wasn't a complete solution. Put a couple of passengers in the back seat of a coil-sprung Brougham and you'll find the tail dragging like a village hot rod.

"Everybody thinks they're wonderful until they have one," comments long-time Cadillac collector Bob Brelsford. Another enthusiast blocks the car up when it is put away in the garage, so the air-bags won't be crimped or cracked with the inevitable leakdown occurs. It pumps back up fast!

Fixing the system—let alone reconverting from a coil-sprung retrofit—is a monumental job, even if you can find the parts. Although air bags have been remanufactured for other Cadillacs, they are not interchangeable with the Eldorado Brougham's.

SUMMARY AND PROSPECTS

Collector emphasis is on the original air-suspended Broughams, despite their poten-

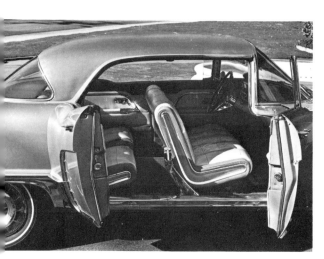

Despite pillarless construction, Broughams generally tend to remain tight, but check for worn rubber door insulation.

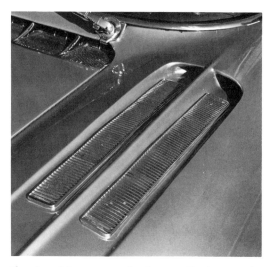

Functional louvers on fenders really do vent the engine, but they are inclined to look rough after years of exposure, and are hard to replace.

tial hazards. These cars carry a strong price premium over coil-spring conversions. Prices for original or fine, restored examples have lately soared to well over $20,000 and are still rising. Prices for lesser examples have leveled off, but you won't find a nice Brougham for much under $15,000, if that.

Even with conventional springs and dragging tails, the Brougham gets many admiring glances, and its owner knows he or she is driving one of the last real factory customs. In sum, this is the hottest single postwar Cadillac model on the collector market today, the most expensive and the most likely to appreciate at a rapid pace in the years ahead. It is the postwar Cadillac for the connoisseur.

PRODUCTION	1957	1958
Model 7059 hardtop sedan	400	304

1957-58 Eldorado Brougham
ENGINE
As per Chapter 17
CHASSIS AND DRIVETRAIN
Transmission: . . . . Hydra-matic
Rear axle ratio: . . . . 3.07:1 (other ratios available)
Rear suspension: . . . . four-link self-leveling with central compressor and air bag units
Front suspension: . . . . . independent self-leveling with air bag units
GENERAL
Wheelbase: . . . . 129.0 in.
Overall length: . . . . 216.3 in.
Track: . . . . 61 in. front and rear
Tire size 8.40x15
Weight: . . . . 5315 lb.
PERFORMANCE
As per Chapter 17

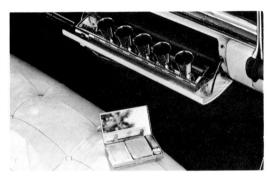

Silver tumblers and lady's compact, original equipment on all Eldorado Broughams, are often missing. Don't even ask the price of replacements on the old-car market today. A four-figure sum is not unusual, and has been paid.

Distinctive Brougham fender badges are another expensive replacement item, not likely to be found as new-old-stock. Fortunately, most are restorable.

Eldorado Brougham town car was the production Brougham's immediate predecessor. A 1955 Motor- ama showcar, it stood only 55 inches high. Most of the styling details were carried over to Broughams.

Chapter 20

Sixty-Special
1957-58

★★

HISTORY

The 1957-58 Sixty-Special was a continuation of the 133-inch-wheelbase Cadillacs, still bearing Fleetwood script, but more of a production car than past Fleetwoods. It was also the first Sixty-Special with four-door pillarless styling, and the first without the identifying vertical louvers that had marked this model since 1942. All in all, the changes worked, at least in 1957, when Cadillac sold a record 24,000 Sixty-Specials. In 1958, however, sales dropped to 12,900. Price may have had something to do with the sales plunge; the basic list price rose $600 in 1958, the first year a Sixty-Special had an entry level over $6,000.

This 1957 Sixty-Special was part of Cadillac's record 24,000-unit production this model year, but has little or no collector following. Rear fender appli-qué was unique to this model—don't ding it, replacements are not obtainable.

IDENTIFICATION

Both years: Broad, ribbed brightmetal trim panels covered lower half of rear fenders. Broad, brightmetal rocker panel moldings. Like the junior four-door hardtops, Sixty-Specials had vent wings at all four corners.

1958: Panels encompassed full fender skirts. Fender bulge above panel received heavier chrome trim.

PERFORMANCE AND UTILITY

At about 5,000 pounds, the 1957-58 Sixty-Special weighed approximately as much as a Sixty-Two convertible and nearly 500 pounds more than a basic hardtop coupe. This made it the poorest performing car in the line, short of the big limousines. But performance wasn't its forte—a smooth, comfortable ride, extra legroom (mainly in the back) and high standards of interior finish were what brought it success in 1957. With excess overhang not only at the ends but at the sides (the driver sits far inboard, as viewed from behind), it was anything but a grand tourer. Built for sedate, quiet motoring, it demands to be driven in the style to which Cadillacs have become accustomed.

PROBLEM AREAS

These are the same as for the 1957-58 Sixty-Two, with the added problem of parts scarcity for unique trim pieces.

SUMMARY AND PROSPECTS

These cars have the same appreciation potential as the 1954-56 Sixty-Specials, although they are somewhat outshown by the flashy Eldorados of these years. Examples can be bought for relatively little money, but appreciation will be modest. As for any such car, collectors should try to get the best example in the most original condition they can find, and not set out determined to have one model year in particular.

PRODUCTION	1957	1958
Model 6039 hardtop sedan	24,000	12,900

1957-58 Sixty-Special
ENGINE
As per Chapter 17
CHASSIS AND DRIVETRAIN
As per Chapter 17
GENERAL
Wheelbase: . . . . 133.0 in.
Overall length: . . . . 1957: 224.4 in.; 1958: 225.3 in.
Track: . . . . 61 in. front and rear
Tire size: 1957: 8.20x15; 1958: 8.00x15
Weight: . . . . 1957: 4735 lb.; 1958: 4930 lb.
PERFORMANCE
As per Chapter 17

An all-time chromemobile, the 1958 Sixty-Special sold in half the quantity of its 1957 predecessor, and is perhaps collectible as a curiosity piece, but for no other reason.

Sixty-Two, DeVille
1959-60

★★★	convertible
★	sedan
★	coupe

HISTORY

H. L. Mencken said, "Nobody ever lost money underestimating the taste of the American public." But there is evidence that GM did just that in 1959. General Motors was profitable—how could it be otherwise?—but not as profitable as it might have been.

The finned behemoths GM built that year saw Chevrolet lose the production race to Ford. Cadillac couldn't help but sell more cars than in recession 1958, but its 1959 model run did not approach its totals in 1957, or even 1956. Of course, a great many other companies built tasteless cars in 1959.

This press photo shows how tailfins had changed in 11 years. Despite regular panning from self-appointed experts, the 1959 was a vastly improved Cadillac with a reliable and important new 390 cid V-8. Collector value is certain.

Perhaps the problem was that GM had lost—temporarily—the styling momentum it had held since the thirties, to a resurgent Chrysler behind design director Virgil Exner. Cadillac's towering 1959 tailfins were a reaction to, not a leading step from, those of Chrysler. Cadillac clay models had been growing tailfins since the first finny Imperial of the 1956 long-leads in June 1955.

The 1959 Cadillac will ever be named to the Ten Worst Cars list of every shallow thinker, largely because of those huge, ungainly, decadent tailfins. On the contrary, it was quite a good car—well built, a smooth performer, good value for the money. As usual it dominated the luxury market, using a new two-pronged attack with the Sixty-Two plus the up-market DeVille. Both models were on a slightly longer wheelbase than in 1958, with a stroked-out 390 cid V-8 packing 325 hp. The convertible came only as a Sixty-Two, but there were Sixty-Two and

Fins looked wildest on the top-down 1959 Sixty-Two convertible; Cadillac suffered from quality problems in 1959 and convertibles can be buckets of bolts, so check any potential buy on rough roads.

The Sixty-Two hardtop for 1959, slightly lower on the price scale from the Coupe de Ville. Two-door roofline gave excellent visibility.

DeVille versions of four- and six-window sedans and the coupe. In a sense the DeVille marked a reincarnation of the old Sixty-One/Sixty-Two relationship, the latter now becoming the price-leader series. Though it started slow, the DeVille eventually outsold the Sixty-Two, which was itself replaced by the Calais in 1965.

The window option was a new twist: The four-window job had a panoramic backlight that much resembled the less expensive GM makes, while the six-window had a flatter backlight with small quarter panes built into the rear-door glassworks. Freon-filled shocks were another unique engineering touch, while air suspension remained ostensibly optional, though not often ordered.

In 1960, the same two-model lineup was continued with no change in specifications or body styles, but the tailfins were greatly pared down to a shape resembling that of the 1957-58 Eldorados. The decision not to try to out-fin Chrysler came in 1957, and Cadillacs of 1960 and beyond continued the trend toward cleaner styling as GM regained the design initiative. Another 1959 styling gimmick that died soon after it appeared was the "rear grille," in which Cadillac applied the same doodads to the under-deck panel as it did to the front end. With hindsight, the 1959 looks pretty horrific to us today. But we should not overreact and condemn the car at large for that. In 1959 the Standard of the World was still the Standard.

IDENTIFICATION

In 1959-60, DeVilles carried a small identifying script on rear fenders above the bright-metal full-length body molding, and had more elaborate interiors.

1959: Unmistakable thin-section, towering tailfins with a pod at mid-height tapering to pairs of elongated, pointed taillights (beloved of customizers and soon seen on everything from Pontiacs to Hanomags). Grille and "rear grille" composed of "floating" chrome buttons. No hood ornament. Much flatter, less prominent arms. V on center of hood. Chrome trim from center of quad lights straight back along top of front fenders.

1960: Somewhat shorter tailfins housing very thin taillights, sprouting from rounded, pontoon-like rear fender. Full-width bumper with ovals at each end housing more lights. Grillework similar to 1959 but no longer bisected by a horizontal bar. Less prominent "rear grille."

PERFORMANCE AND UTILITY

A couple hundred pounds added weight was offset by the new 10.25:1 compression, 325 hp 390 V-8, giving the 1959 plenty of urge at the expense of gas mileage. This was a fine new engine, too, and the best ohv to

Six-window version of Sixty-Two sedan for 1959. The four-window type had the "shelf-back" extensively wrapped rear window of other GM makes.

This variation had much higher production, so the four-window is the type to look for.

date from Cadillac. Surprisingly, though, these cars were a fraction of an inch shorter than the 1958, and no wider. Otherwise, they performed the same as the 1957-58 models.

PROBLEM AREAS

The 390 is recognized as one of Cadillac's better ohv V-8s of the early postwar period, but there were other problems with this generation. Front ends were notorious for vibration and chatter. One collector recalls a company report about them entitled something like "Rattles, shakes, sonic booms and things that go bump in the night." For that reason, front ends deserve close scrutiny before you purchase. Afterward, you should lay in a supply of new-old-stock or reproduction bushings, tie rods ends and so on.

Another very serious problem from 1959 on was rust, which seriously affects these cars after long lives in the nothern salt belts. Those equipped with air suspension offer the hazards cited for the 1957-58 Sixty-Special, though replacement air bags for non-Eldo Broughams are on the market. These cars are like the contemporary Studebaker Hawks; you can drive the engine and chassis forever while the body disappears into the ground around you.

SUMMARY AND PROSPECTS

Though collectibility of the late fifties and early sixties Cadillacs has grown slowly, the 1959 model (convertible in particular) has become a sort of cult car. Many otherwise-sane enthusiasts own one as an expression of defiance—others because they're nostalgic for the "space ship era" of automotive design. There are few neutrals on the sub-

---

1959-60 Sixty-Two, DeVille
ENGINE
Type: . . . . 8-cylinder 90° V-type, watercooled, cast iron block and heads
Bore x stroke: . . . . 4.00x3.88 in.
Displacement: . . . . 390.0 ci
Valve operation: . . . . overhead, pushrod actuated
Compression ratio: 10.5:1
Carburetion: . . . . Carter #2814S 2bbl
Bhp: . . . . 325 bhp gross at 4800 rpm
CHASSIS AND DRIVETRAIN
As per Chapter 17
GENERAL
Wheelbase: . . . . 130.0 in.
Overall length: . . . . 225.0 in.
Track: . . . . 61 in. front and rear
Tire size: 8.00x15
Weight: . . . . 4690-5455 lb.
PERFORMANCE
Acceleration: . . . . 0-60: 11.5 seconds; 0-100: 34.0 seconds
Top speed: . . . . 118-122 mph
Fuel mileage: . . . . 10-16 mpg

Base-line Sixty-Two coupe for 1960 was again a less-expensive version of Coupe de Ville. The 1960 model was priced considerably lower, car for car, than the 1959; the latter may be controversial, but it's also distinctive, and that's a never-fail key to collectibility.

ject of 1959s; you either love them or loathe them. Some Cadillac collectors willing to overlook their styling excesses have problems with the cheaper materials used in their make-up: "There was a lot of printed alumi-num trim that just looks tacky, especially with age," commented Bud Juneau.

Because they were overt products of their age, the rocketships will probably emerge with more appeal than the design generations on either side of them. For the moment, 1960 is not outlandishly priced, but an awful lot of people want a 1959, and convertibles have no trouble drawing five-figure bids. A lot to pay for decadence!

Cadillac cut tailfins in a hurry in 1960, also cleaned up rear dummy grille, but cars were quite similar.

PRODUCTION: DeVILLE	*1959*	*1960*
Model 6329		
hardtop sedan 6-window	19,158	22,579
Model 6337		
hardtop coupe	21,924	21,585
Model 6339		
hardtop sedan 4-window	12,308	9,225
SIXTY-TWO	*1959*	*1960*
Model 6229		
hardtop sedan 6-window	23,461	26,824
Model 6237		
hardtop coupe	21,947	19,978
Model 6239		
hardtop sedan 4-window	14,138	9,984
Model 6267		
convertible coupe	11,130	14,000
Bare chassis and export	60	38

Chapter 22

Eldorado
1959-60

★★★★ Biarritz convertible
★★★ Seville coupe

HISTORY

More of a conventional Cadillac than at any other time in its history, the limited-production Eldorado used the same body styling as the junior models, although for the first time it was broken out under a separate "64" numerical model designation. The difference was now mainly in chrome and trim—plus a standard performance engine with three two-barrel carburetors and 345 hp (optional on Sixty-Two and DeVille). Air suspension was now standardized on all Eldorados. Other standard items were Autronic Eye headlamp dimming, automatic Cruise Control and power door locks. Sevilles featured a fabric-covered roof, color keyed to the interior.

Though $100 cheaper than the year before, Eldos cost a staggering amount ($7,400), and sales were miniscule at just over 2,000. In 1960, the price remained unchanged but only a few more were sold, and more convertibles than coupes. Probably for this reason Cadillac discontinued the Seville hardtop after 1960, producing only ragtop Eldorados through 1966.

IDENTIFICATION

1959: Wide brightmetal trim running full length from front wheels back to tail, sweeping upward and then forward along base of fins and on through beltline. Eldorado name in small block letters on lower front fenders.
1960: Similar treatment, with addition of

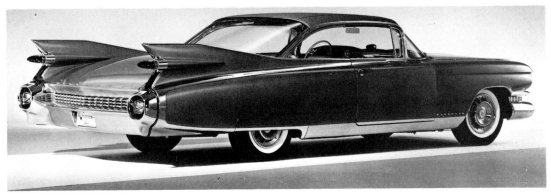

Just a gussied-up standard hardtop, the 1959 Eldorado relied mainly on brightwork and the 345 hp engine as standard for its modicum of luxury compared to regular Cadillacs. The 1959 tailfins were the same as the rest of the line.

chrome outline molding along top edge of tailfins. Eldorado nameplate moved to front fenders.

Sevilles carried color-keyed fabric tops both years.

PERFORMANCE AND UTILITY

This was a very hot Cadillac with the standard tri-carb 345 V-8, but a very heavy one with about 5,000 pounds to shove off the line. It was no larger than the 1957-58 generation despite having swoopier lines, so it might just fit in your garage. The 1959-60 Eldo is a handful except on the straightaways, and capable of returning under 10 mpg in traffic. The car's many power accessories make managing it easy, as long as it's not pressed.

PROBLEM AREAS

Problems with the 1959-60 Sixty-Two also appear with the Eldorado, with the added caveat of hard-to-find Eldorado-only trim components. The standard air suspension is inclined to leak and may have been replaced by conventional suspension on many examples.

SUMMARY AND PROSPECTS

About the only way to one-up the owner of a 1959 De Ville, the Eldorado leads the junior models in value and appreciation through its extreme rarity. Very definitely the best investment you can make among 1959 Cadillacs, except for the Eldorado Brougham.

PRODUCTION	1959	1960
Model 6437		
Seville hardtop	975	1,075
Model 6467		
Biarritz convertible	1,320	1,285

1959-60 Eldorado
ENGINE
Type: . . . . 8-cylinder 90° V-type, watercooled, cast iron block and heads
Bore x stroke: . . . . 4.00x3.88 in.
Displacement: . . . . 390.0 ci
Valve operation: . . . . overhead, pushrod actuated
Compression ratio: 10.5:1
Carburetion: . . . . three Rochester #7015901 2bbl
Bhp: . . . . 345 bhp gross at 4800 rpm
CHASSIS AND DRIVETRAIN
As per Chapter 17
GENERAL
Wheelbase: . . . . 130.0 in.
Overall length: . . . . 225.0 in.
Track: . . . . 61 in. front and rear
Tire size: 8.20x15
Weight: . . . . 4855-5060 lb.
PERFORMANCE
Acceleration: . . . . 0-60: 10.5 seconds
Top speed: . . . . 120-125 mph
Fuel mileage: . . . . 8-14 mpg

Eldorado's disappearing top was still a feature; interiors were ultra-posh with individual front seats.

Eldorado Biarritz followed other 1960 Cadillacs in deemphasizing tailfins, but was even less distinctive as the premium model than it was in 1959. Wide brightmetal rocker trim is impossible to find; all chromework on any potential purchase ought to be in excellent shape.

Eldorado Brougham 1959-60

★★★★

HISTORY

Cadillac kept the Brougham in the line in 1959 and 1960, but farmed out its construction to Pininfarina in Torino. Far less different than in 1957-58, at a glance these Broughams are hard to differentiate from conventional junior models. Though they shared the new 130-inch wheelbase with their linemates, the Broughams had unique sheet metal which is not interchangeable.

Within the context of the times, Pininfarina and Cadillac kept the Brougham restrained. It was the ony 1959 model that lacked the gross tailfins and bullet taillights; indeed, its styling closely prefigured that of the 1960 Cadillac line. The roofline, too, was different: crisp and formal rather than rounded, without the severely wrapped windshield and dogleg A-post of the standard models. This too was a statement of things to come from a more conservative minded Cadillac in the sixties.

These Eldorado Broughams are extremely rare today, as only 200 were built. The model was dropped as a net loss to the Division after 1960, though the Brougham name was established and later replaced the Seventy-Five designation.

IDENTIFICATION

1959: Only model without bullet taillights, high tailfins and wraparound windshield. Thin bodyside molding but relatively conservative brightmetal decoration except up front. Lacks large, horizontal grille-bisecting bar.

Pininfarina built the body for the 1959 Eldorado Brougham, which was far less different from standard than 1957-58 Broughams had been, and also sold for less, though even fewer were built. The Brougham experiment had cost Cadillac about $10 for every dollar it made.

1960: Pininfarina badge removed. Hubcaps changed to slightly smaller dish design than 1959. Cloisonne emblems on rear of rear fenders. Creaseline in lower body sides. Stock grillework but again the only Cadillac without wrapped windshield and dogleg post.

Narrow-band whitewalls both years were a Brougham-only feature.

PERFORMANCE AND UTILITY

There was little difference between this Brougham and the 1959-60 Biarritz/Seville, aside from two extra doors. These cars performed, rode and handled the same. All 1959-60 Eldorados originally shared the standard air suspension, but many have had it replaced during their lifetimes. The most conservative-looking Cadillacs of this vintage, they are thus more timelessly styled. But they are quite a bucket of bolts compared to the more carefully assembled, Detroit-built 1957-58 Broughams.

PROBLEM AREAS

The Italians were given to using a lot of filler in bodywork, and rust is a definite hazard on these Broughams. There is also a dearth of replacement body panels, since only 200 cars were built and the panels don't interchange with those on other Cadillacs.

SUMMARY AND PROSPECTS

In the opinion of many Cadillac experts, the 1959-60 Eldorado Broughams are two great "sleepers" among postwar Cadillacs—

very underrated by the collector community. They do not carry Milestone status, and are far less unique than the 1957-58 series which everybody wants. But they have a great deal to recommend them: They're far scarcer than the 1957-58 models; they're custom-built (admittedly with a lot of Italian bondo); they're really good looking compared to other Cadillacs of this generation, with their formal, squared-off rooflines; and they're fine road cars. They compare to the 1957-58s much as the Mercedes-Benz 190SL compares to the 300SL: quite nice in their own way, just overshadowed by something else a lot more exotic. Look for them.

PRODUCTION	*1959*	*1960*
Model 6929 hardtop sedan	99	101

1959-60 Eldorado Brougham
ENGINE
As per Chapter 22
CHASSIS AND DRIVETRAIN
Transmission: . . . . Hydra-matic
Rear axle ratio: 3.21:1
Rear suspension: . . . . four-link self-leveling with central compressor and air bag units
Front suspension: . . . . independent self-leveling with air units
GENERAL
Wheelbase: . . . . 130.0 in.
Overall length: . . . . 225.0 in.
Track: . . . . 61 in. front and rear
Tire size: 1959: 8.40x15; 1960: 8.20x15
Weight: . . . . 5200 lb. est.
PERFORMANCE
As per Chapter 22

Pininfarina's badge is visible on rear fender of this 1959 Eldorado Brougham. This is the only 1959 without the vast fins. The 1960 was unchanged.

Chapter 24

Sixty-Special
1959-60

HISTORY

For the first time since 1941, the Fleetwood Sixty-Sixty special rode the same wheelbase as the junior models—no longer the posh owner-driver semilimo of the past, but a conventional Cadillac with more fads, frills and fancy stuff. Though it cost no more than the 1958 version, it failed to meet the very low 1958 sales level—perhaps for this reason: Cadillac actually had the chutzpah to call it "tasteful and restrained' in press releases, but there wasn't much to do without and exclusive wheelbase, other that add gook.

The 1960 version was just more of the same, and sales were even lower. But there were definite improvements: cleaner lines without the huge tailfins, leather-grained fabric roof covering, and a bow toward tradition with the return of the vertical louvers of 1942-56. (This time there were six of them, placed far back on the rear fender.) Both Sixty-Specials in these two years were six-window, pillarless hardtops.

IDENTIFICATION

1959: Heavy, sculpted convex panel within tapering body creaselines, starting with scoop on door and narrowing to point at far rear.

1960: Six vertical louvers on extreme rear fenders. Fabric-covered top.

Sixty-Special for 1959 was a rolling jukebox, and is little noticed by collectors today. It had little, save useless extra trim items to distinguish it; shared standard six-window body with less expensive models.

In general, styling for both years followed that of junior models.

PERFORMANCE AND UTILITY

The 1959-60 Sixty-Special had little to recommend it this time, except the solid 390 cid V-8 which was all-new to Cadillac in 1959. It was about 120 pounds heavier than the Sixty-Two six-window sedan it resembled, much of that apparently in chrome-plated ornamentation. A jumbo whale-mobile that was no fun to drive then, it is less fun today. In addition, with the 390 V-8, Cadillacs began to require a near-total diet of leaded premium fuel, something that's hard to find today and destined to become even more scarce.

PROBLEM AREAS

These cars shared all problems with the other 1959-60 models.

SUMMARY AND PROSPECTS

One of the least collectible Sixty-Specials, and beset with the same problem areas that attend other, more desirable models from these two years, the 1959-60 Sixty-Special is going nowhere fast on the market. However, a nice, clean original one might be quite a bargain.

PRODUCTION	1959	1960
Model 6039		
hardtop sedan		
6-window	12,250	11,800

1959-60 Sixty-Special
ENGINE
As per Chapter 21
CHASSIS AND DRIVETRAIN
Transmission: . . . . Hydra-matic
Rear axle ratio: . . . . 2.94:1, optional 3.21:1
Rear suspension: . . . . live axle, helical coil springs, tube shocks
Front suspension: . . . . independent, coil springs, tube shocks
Air suspension: . . . . optional: central compressor and accumulator, self leveling, with four-link rear suspension and air units or coil springs
GENERAL
Wheelbase: . . . . 130.0 in.
Overall length: . . . . 225.0 in.
Track: . . . . 61 in. front and rear
Tire size: 8.00x15
Weight: . . . . 4880-4890 lb.
PERFORMANCE
As per Chapter 21

Little except a trim shuffle occurred on the Sixty-Special for 1960. Upper trim line was moved higher and traditional hashmarks returned.

Sixty-Two, DeVille
1961-64

★★★ convertible
★★ Town Sedan
★★ Park Avenue
★ other models

HISTORY

Retaining the basic 1959-60 shell, Cadillac came up with a handsome facelift for 1961—that greatly improved styling but didn't quite overcome the bad taste in people's mouths after two years of excess—and sold slightly fewer cars in 1961 than in 1960. The two look-alike models shared the same relationship as before: The Sixty-Two had the sole convertible, and each model included two sedans and a hardtop coupe.

A special 1961 Sixty-Two was the Town Sedan, or "short-deck," apparently designed to win over the few Cadillac people attracted to the compact car craze. Cadillac charged a premium for this plucked chicken, and for

that reason alone it didn't appeal. But management added another short-deck in 1962 (this time to the De Ville series, calling it the Park Avenue) and priced both short-decks the same as the more conventional models. The Park Avenue didn't sell, either, though the new formal, squarish roofline made it look a lot better. After a handful of 1963 DeVille Park Avenues were flogged, Cadillac gave them up for lost.

The big sellers were the conventional long-decks (both four- and six-window) and the hardtop. Even the Sixty-Two convertible did well, selling at a profitable clip of about 18,000 annually.

Under the leadership of Bill Mitchell, GM

Four-window Sedan de Ville had stylish formal rear roofline, was an extremely popular 1963 model, and is liked by collectors of big Cadillacs today. Look for the cleanest original you can find.

was rapidly reassuming the design lead from Chrysler, and styling just kept getting better. A crisp, extruded look was now in vogue, and Mitchell kept only enough tailfin for tradition's sake. Detail changes were very minor, though under the skin things were happening. The 1963 models saw the last of the old Hydra-matic, and 1964 brought in the new, much more flexible and capable Turbo Hydra-matic. In 1964, extremism in the defense of Cadillac was no vice as far as engines went, and the 390 V-8 gave way to a monster 429—more powerful, but an oil burner. Vinyl roofs appeared that year, too, along with a complicated but effective thermostatically controlled Comfort Control heating/air-conditioning system. Factory air was installed on seventy-five percent of the cars.

IDENTIFICATION

Identifying script for DeVilles.

1961: An all-new, up-to-date body, with cleaner greenhouse and creaselines on the fuselage. Ovoid taillamp housings were now placed on their sides. Round parking lights. Neat grille extending between headlights only, peaked horizontally in the middle.

1962: Simpler grillework, bisected horizontally by a slim bar. Oblong parking lights. Lower rear fins. Cadillac script mounted on lower-right-hand corner of grillework. Closed, formal roofline on four-window models, wrapped backlight having been eliminated. Vertical ovoid lights at rear.

1963: Body sides smoothed out. Creaselines either eliminated or softened. Parking lights carried above bumper in small grilles matching main grille, which was busier. Narrow standup ovals housing each pair of rear lights. Taillights still in fins.

1964: Simpler grille, composed to emphasize the horizontal, peaked both vertically and horizontally. Still-lower tailfins. Horizontal grille bar painted body color. Rear bumper ending with squarer lines, and vee'd vertically.

PERFORMANCE AND UTILITY

The smoother-shifting, more flexible three-speed Turbo Hydra-matic was a major improvement in 1964, giving Cadillac even more silkiness than it had before, and was easily capable of handling the more powerful 1964 engine. The wheelbase was shorter by only half an inch from 1959-60, and the cars

The 1964 Coupe de Ville, a sporty and stylish big Cadillac, had still smaller tailfins and a more horizontal grille, plus other detail improvements. Its big, new 429 engine was an oil burner, though.

Sedan de Ville for 1964, changed only in detail; the four-window version was the top-selling single body style in Cadillac's line. In the mid-sixties, four-window models were prettier. They are more popular with collectors today.

were only fractionally lighter, but they seemed to handle better and ride just as well. Fuel thirst goes without saying and, like the 390, the 429 required leaded premium fuel.

PROBLEM AREAS

While the new automatic transmission solved any lingering problems in that department, the 429 engine was not one of Cadillac's better efforts. It was famous for its oil consumption, and restorers say it also doesn't respond well to rebuilds, which often end in cylinder-wall distortion. The 429 persisted until 1968, and it is not looked upon with fondness. From 1963 up, front coil springs often collapse with age, an embarrassment to Cadillac, and to you; so fix them.

SUMMARY AND PROSPECTS

The oldest Cadillacs that still look contemporary—albeit big—by today's standards, these were well-built, tastefully executed land cruisers with much to recommend them for comfort, convenience and effortless motoring. They haven't exactly been dynamite among collectors yet, but that may have to do with chronology. Just about the time collectors began to look beyond the fifties for their cars the energy crisis hit, and what followed has not been very conducive to owning a big, premium-fuel Caddy. These cars have not appreciated much, allowing for inflation, and there are many bargains to be had. They also won't appreciate any faster in the future. Short-decks may do a bit better, being scarce.

1961-64 Sixty-Two
ENGINE
Type: .... 8-cylinder 90° V-type, watercooled, cast iron block and heads
Bore x stroke: .... 1961-63: 4.00x3.88 in.; 1964: 4.13x4.00 in.
Displacement: .... 1961-63: 390.0 ci; 1964: 429.0 ci
Valve operation: .... overhead, pushrod actuated
Compression ratio: 10.5:1
Carburetion: ..... 1961-63: Rochester #701930 4bbl; 1964: Carter #3655S 4bbl
Bhp: .... 1961-63: 325 bhp at 4800 rpm; 1964: 340 bhp at 4600 rpm (gross)
CHASSIS AND DRIVETRAIN
Transmission: .... Hydra-matic
Rear axle ratio: .... 2.94:1, 3.21:1 optional in 1961
Rear suspension: .... live axle, helical coil rubberized springs, tube shocks
Front suspension: .... independent, rubberized coil springs, tube shocks
Air suspension: .... dropped
GENERAL
Wheelbase: .... 129.5 in.
Overall length: .... standard: 223-223.5 in.; short-deck: 215.0 in.
Track: .... 61 in. front and rear
Tire size: 8.00x15
Weight: .... 4475-4720 lb.
PERFORMANCE (1964)
Acceleration: .... 0-60: 9.8 seconds; 0-100: 17.5 seconds
Top speed: .... 120-122 mph
Fuel mileage: .... 10-14 mpg

PRODUCTION: SIXTY-TWO

	1961	1962	1963	1964
Model 6229 hardtop sedan 6-window	26,216	16,730	12,929	9,243
Model 6237* hardtop coupe	16,005	16,833	17,786	12,166
Model 6239 hardtop sedan 4-window	4,700	17,314	16,980	13,670
Model 6267 convertible	15,500	16,800	17,600	17,900
Model 6299 Town Sedan 6-window	3,756	2,600	—	—
Bare chassis	5	—	3	—

PRODUCTION: DeVILLE

	1961	1962	1963	1964
Model 6329 hardtop sedan 6-window	26,415	16,230	15,146	14,627
Model 6337* hardtop coupe	20,156	25,675	31,749	38,195
Model 6389 Park Avenue sedan 6-window	—	2,600	1,575	—

* Designations changed to 6247/6347 in 1962 and 6257/6357 in 1963-64.

Chapter 26

Eldorado
1961-66

★★★↲

HISTORY

Cadillac probably kept the Eldorado going in the early sixties more for its image than its profits. Though the Seville coupe was dropped with this styling generation, the convertible hadn't sold much better and improved only gradually. Its gains probably came from those who would have bought a closed Eldo, if one were offered. The decision to pare its price by about $1,000 in 1961 and make it far less unique apparently backfired. This move ran smack into Bill Mitchell's determination to throw away all the chrome and gook that had served to make Eldos stand out in the past, so it came away looking rather plain.

Aesthetically this was a plus because, like all Cadillacs, it just kept looking more elegant as the years went by.

In 1964 the Eldorado formally became a Fleetwood; although the meaning of that term had all but vanished, it was still good for a few hundred extra sales. Through 1966 it ran as a sporty linemate to that other owner-driver Fleetwood, the Sixty-Special, and both models were mightily improved from their gaudy days in the late fifties. Eldos were priced only about $1,000 higher than the standard convertibles, most of it going into more deluxe trim and a raft of standard accessories.

First year for Eldorado as an official Fleetwood body was 1966. By this time, Bill Mitchell's leadership had ended all traces of the overdecorated past. Convertibles only were offered, but they are the leading body style to collect.

IDENTIFICATION

1961: Biarritz script on forward end of front fenders. Designated in 63 series, but not a DeVille.

1962: Bodyside molding similar to that of 1960, but finely done and clean. Bucket seats optional. Seven choices of Cannes cloth and leather interiors.

1963: Trimmed like the Sixty-Special. Clean sides with no chrome moldings. Eldorado name in block letters on lower fenders behind front wheelwells. Cadillac arms and laurel wreath on rear fenders.

1964: Similar styling, but now the only Cadillac with fully open rear wheels and called a Fleetwood, not a Biarritz.

1965: Restyled with the rest of the line. Again resembled the clean-sided Sixty-Special with script unchanged on fenders. Bench or bucket seats offered.

1966: Similarly styled, again with Eldorado script.

Shared styling with Calais and DeVille in 1965 and 1966.

1961-66 Eldorado

ENGINE

Type: . . . . 8-cylinder 90° V-type, watercooled, cast iron block and heads
Bore x stroke: . . . . . . 1961-63: 4.00x3.88 in.; 1964-66: 4.13x4.00 in.
Displacement: . . . . 1961-63: 390.0 ci; 1964-66: 429.0 ci
Valve operation: . . . . overhead, pushrod actuated
Compression ratio: 10.5:1
Carburetion: . . . . . 1961-63: Rochester #701930 4bbl; 1964: Carter #3655S 4bbl; 1965-66: Rochester #7026030 4bbl
Bhp: . . . . . 1961-63: 325 bhp at 4800 rpm; 1964-66: 340 bhp at 4600 rpm (gross)

CHASSIS AND DRIVETRAIN

Transmission: . . . . . . 1961-63: Hydra-matic; 1964-66: Turbo Hydra-matic 3-speed
Rear axle ratio: . . . . 2.94:1; other ratios optional
Rear suspension: . . . . . live axle, helical rubberized coil springs, tube shocks
Front suspension: . . . . independent, coil springs, tube shocks
Frame: . . . . 1961-64: X-type backbone; 1965-66: full perimeter with automatic level control
Air suspension: . . . . dropped

GENERAL

Wheelbase: . . . . 129.5 in.
Overall length: . . . . 224-225.5 in.
Track: . . . . 1961-64: 61 in. front and rear; 1965-66: 62.5 in. front and rear
Tire size: 1961-63: 8.00x15; 1964: 8.20x15; 1965-66: 9.00x15
Weight: . . . . 4500-4660 lb.

PERFORMANCE (1964-66)

As per Chapter 25

PERFORMANCE AND UTILITY

The 1961-66 Eldorado performed and handled like the 1961-64 Sixty-Two and DeVille.

PROBLEM AREAS

The Eldorado also had the same problem areas as the Sixty-Two and DeVille, plus the added problem of finding special Eldo-only trim, which is extremely scarce.

SUMMARY AND PROSPECTS

This is not as "loud" a car as Eldorados of the past, and far more timeless as a result, but it is overshadowed in the field by the radical front-drive successor of 1967. It is a bit of a sleeper for these reasons, but as satisfying a big convertible as you can find, provided you don't mind seeking out premium fuel and a little bit of tetraethyl lead. The 1961-66 Eldorado is probably destined to gain quite a bit in value due to its extreme scarcity, but this factor is partly negated by its character as one of the dinosaurs, a car increasingly impractical to run.

The 1966 Eldorado had a restyled deck lid, new lighting at outer edges of bumpers, new rear bumper with lower half painted body color (making restorations easier). It was the last rear-drive Eldorado, available only as convertible. Historically important, it is the best investment among Eldos in this chapter.

PRODUCTION	1961	1962	1963
Model 6267 Biarritz convertible	1,450	1,450	1,825
	1964	1965	1966
Model 6367 convertible	1,870	2,125	2,250

Chapter 27

Sixty-Special
1961-65

★★⌐

HISTORY

The 1961-65 Sixty-Special made a major comeback for the up-market sedan, reflecting the fine new early-sixties styling of conservative elegance. It once again accounted for close to 15,000 units per year by 1964, and over 18,000 in 1965. The old, Chevy-like greenhouse vanished on the 1961 model, which had a formal rear roof quarter with convertiblelike creasing, covered in a leatherlike material. The small, private rear window was surrounded in a molding of body color rather than chrome to heighten the feel of a limousine. This was really the spiritual successor to the now-defunct Eldorado Brougham; indeed, there would be a new Brougham in this series starting with 1966 models.

Sixty-Special styling was similarly handled through 1965, though for some reason the 1964 seemed a bit gorpy looking. Always built on the standard junior wheelbase, the Sixty-Special of these years won sales for its quiet opulence, quality of workmanship and silence in motion. A nice car!

IDENTIFICATION

1961: Formal roofline with crease and leatherlike covering, color-keyed rear window molding. Six slender, vertical bars at ends of rear fenders.

1962: Traditional bars shifted to roof

One of the best Sixty-Special models of the decade was the 1963; hashmarks had returned to the rear roof pillar, which was formal again. Too thirsty to ever become popular with collectors, otherwise a very nice Cadillac in every way.

quarters. Small red cloisonne emblems on lower front fenders.

1963: Only five bars in the same spot. Cloisonne emblems removed.

1964: Heavier looking, thanks to broad lower-body brightmetal (they couldn't seem to get it out of their system!). Vertical louvers vanished. Laurel wreath and Cadillac arms moved into their place on rear roof quarters.

1965: Return to traditional B-pillar sedan construction and styling that closely resembled junior models.

PERFORMANCE AND UTILITY

These cars handled and performed like the 1961-64 Sixty-Two and DeVille.

PROBLEM AREAS

In addition to sharing problems with the 1961-64 Sixty-Two and DeVille, the relatively few unique Sixty-Special trim parts are scarce.

SUMMARY AND PROSPECTS

This was a really fine Cadillac in every way except perhaps the 429 engine, which had its bad points. However, like the junior models of this period, it faces an uncertain future due to its high thirst and demand for leaded super. It is more desirable than the Sixty-Two and DeVille, and usually slightly more expensive. There is some chance for gradual appreciation, though not as rapid as the later Fleetwood Broughams.

1961-65 Sixty-Special
ENGINE
Type: . . . . 8-cylinder 90° V-type, watercooled, cast iron block and heads
Bore x stroke: . . . . . . 1961-63: 4.00x3.88 in.; 1964-65: 4.13x4.00 in.
Displacement: . . . . 1961-63: 390.0 ci; 1964-65: 429.0 ci
Valve operation: . . . . overhead, pushrod actuated
Compression ratio: 10.5:1
Carburetion: . . . . . 1961-63: Rochester #701930 4bbl; 1964: Carter #2655S 4bbl; 1965: Rochester #7026030 4bbl
Bhp: . . . . . 1961-63: 325 bhp at 4800 rpm; 1964-65: 340 bhp at 4600 rpm (gross)
CHASSIS AND DRIVETRAIN
As per Chapter 26
GENERAL
Wheelbase: . . . . 1961-64: 129.5 in.; 1965: 133.0 in.
Overall length: . . . . 1961-64: 224-225.5 in.; 1965: 227.5 in.
Track: . . . 1961-64: 61 in. front and rear; 1965: 62.5 in. front and rear
Tire size: 8.00x15
Weight: . . . . 4615-4770 lb.
PERFORMANCE (1964-65)
As per Chapter 25

PRODUCTION	*1961*	*1962*	*1963*	*1964*	*1965*
Model 6039 sedan*	15,500	13,350	14,000	14,550	18,100

*68069 in 1965

The 1964 Fleetwood Sixty-Special four-window sedan, with Fleetwood crest shifted to roof quarters.

Chapter 28

Calais, DeVille
1965-70

★★ Convertible
★ Other Models

HISTORY

We come here to the borderline of Cadillac collectibility; the first edition of this book was concerned only with post-1970 cars having collector potential. This just barely applies to the restyled line of Junior Cadillacs that arrived in 1965, and really only to the ever-popular convertible—still produced at a rate of over 15,000 per year through 1970.

Cadillac had a resounding near-200,000-car year in 1965, when the long-running Sixty-Two was finally put to rest in favor of a new price leader called Calais. This time,

though, the up-market DeVille got the convertible body style, and the Calais gradually faded away, much as had the old Sixty-One in the early fifties. The major styling changes for 1965 were longer, lower silhouette and the disappearance of tailfins. Rear styling consisted of a straight bumper and vertical lamp clusters, flush-top contour on rear quarter panels and curved side windows. Horsepower went up to 340, giving Cadillac the highest power-to-weight ratio in the industry. All models except the Seventy-Five had dual-driving-range Turbo Hydra-

The 1965 Calais was smoothly styled, typically Mitchellesque, but sold in lower quantities than DeVille. It therefore may be worth more collector interest, though collectibility is not high in this area.

matic and a perimeter frame; all had a soni-cally balanced exhaust system.

Automatic level control was an important improvement in 1965; variable-ratio power steering in 1966; printed circuits in 1967. In 1968, emission laws saw the problem-prone 429 replaced with a much better but even larger 472 V-8, putting out 375 bhp. This time Cadillac took no chances: The 472 was extensively proven over half a million miles. Other 1968 features were hidden wind-shield wipers and a bunch of government-mandated safety equipment.

In 1969, Cadillac produced a record 266,798 units for the calendar year and elim-inated front vent windows—one guess as to which fact is more important to collectors. In 1970, all models had energy-absorbing steer-ing columns, push-button seat-belt buckles, shoulder harnesses and other safety gad-gets. Stylewise, the 1970 changes were a grille with bright vertical accents over a cross-hatch pattern, new horizontal chrome trim on parking lights, winged crests instead of Vs on hoods, and new taillamps.

IDENTIFICATION

1965: Wide, fine-mesh grille and vertical quad headlamps with recessed parking lights.

1966: Same basic layout with coarser mesh and a central horizontal bar. Oblong parking lights set into grille.

1967: Forward-leaning front fenders and grillework. Revised rear fenders with large vertical caps containing all lights.

1968: Longer hood, with central portion raised, tapering to fine-mesh grille with raised center section (returning to an old tradition).

1969: Vent panes eliminated. Finer-mesh grille. Forward-leaning front end dropped. Redesign along more formal lines.

1970: Long-running V emblem dropped from hoods and decks, arms and laurel wreath remaining. Finer-mesh grille.

PERFORMANCE AND UTILITY

Much the same comments apply here as to the 1961-64 generation of volume Cadillacs, but increasing driveability problems oc-curred once car design began to be influ-enced by mandates from Washington in 1968. Nevertheless, the 472 V-8 coped ably with most emission regulations of those days. The problem was that this was still very much a premium-fuel engine, and we'd have to wait for its replacement by an unleaded drinker. The sheer bulk and run-

Only details were changed for 1966, and Calais retained the Cadillac 429 V-8 with 340 horsepower. Obvious styling shift was at front fender, where cornering light was placed, separate from bumper.

Triple-band narrow whitewalls could be hard to duplicate today; given current collector interest, don't bother.

ning costs of these cars will probably prevent their ever being gathered in numbers, except for the convertibles.

PROBLEM AREAS

The 1967 models had the same old 429 that had troubled owners before, but there were changes to the rocker arms and improvements in the piston ring area. Still, the 1967 was considered piggish by some owners, due to the enormous overload of accessories and power equipment. The 1968 had a much better 472 engine with individual rockers. The 1969 model seems quicker than the 1968 to some collectors, but they also admit that the

Mute testimony as to why it doesn't pay to restore sixties Cadillacs is this 1968 DeVille convertible, with acres of plastic, vinyl or leather upholstery, plus its complicated, accessory-laden cockpit. The thing to do, if you must have one, is to find an exceptional, low-mileage original.

1965-70 Calais, DeVille

ENGINE

Type: . . . . 8-cylinder 90° V-type, watercooled, cast iron block and heads
Bore x stroke: . . . . . 1965-67: 4.13x4.00 in.; 1968-70: 4.30x4.06 in.
Displacement: . . . . 1965-67: 429.0 ci; 1968-70: 472.0 ci
Valve operation: . . . . overhead, pushrod actuated
Compression ratio: 10.5:1
Carburetion: . . . 1966: Rochester #701930 4bbl; 1967-70: Rochester Quadra-Jet #7028230 4bbl
Bhp: . . . . . 1965-67: 340 bhp at 4600 rpm; 1968-70: 375 bhp at 4400 rpm (gross)

CHASSIS AND DRIVETRAIN

Transmission: . . . . Turbo Hydra-matic
Rear axle ratio: . . . . 2.94:1; optional 3.21:1
Rear suspension: . . . . live axle, coil springs, tube shocks
Front suspension: . . . . independent, coil springs, tube shocks
Frame: . . . . full perimeter

GENERAL

Wheelbase: . . . . 129.5 in.
Overall length: . . . . 225.0 in.
Track: . . . . 62.5 in. front and rear
Tire size: 1965-69: 9.00x15; 1970: L78x15
Weight: . . . . 4390-4725 lb.

PERFORMANCE

Acceleration: . . . . . 0-80: 15.5 seconds, 17.5 seconds from 1968-on
Top speed: . . . . 120-125 mph
Fuel mileage: . . . . 12-15 mpg

The 1968 Sedan de Ville was Cadillac's best-selling single model that year, at 72,662 units, and is one of the least collectible. All 1968s carried the mammoth new 472 cid V-8 with 375 (gross) horsepower—a smooth and reliable gas guzzler.

standards of trim and quality took a definite nose dive that year. We were rapidly moving out of the age of craftsmanship and toward the era of plastique.

SUMMARY AND PROSPECTS

These are cars that time has passed by, still no doubt hankered after in places where roads are straight and gas pumps handy. It is impossible to forecast any appreciation for these models, always excepting the convertible—but even that barely makes the cut among car enthusiasts. A good buy if you find a nice, clean, inexpensive example, but for heaven's sake don't spend any money restoring one.

PRODUCTION: CALAIS	1965	1966	1967	1968	1969	1970
Model 68239* hardtop sedan	13,975	13,025	9,880	10,025	6,825	5,187
Model 68257* hardtop coupe	12,515	11,080	9,085	8,165	5,600	4,724
Model 68269 four-door sedan	7,721	4,575	2,865	——	——	——

PRODUCTION: DeVILLE	1965	1966	1967	1968	1969	1970
Model 68339* hardtop sedan	45,535	60,550	59,902	72,662	72,958	83,274
Model 68357* hardtop coupe	43,345	50,580	52,905	63,935	65,755	76,043
Model 68367 convertible	19,200	19,200	18,202	18,025	16,445	15,172
Model 68369 four-door sedan	15,000	11,860	8,800	9,850	7,890	7,230

*Designations changed to 68249/68349 for hardtop sedan and 68247/68347 for hardtop coupe commencing 1967.

Slowly but surely the glitz was going; big still, though. This is a 1970 model year two-door Coupe de Ville. Considerable airbrush work has been done on this factory photograph to smooth the lines.

Chapter 29

Sixty-Special
1966-70

> ★★★ **Fleetwood Brougham**
> ★ **four-door sedan**

HISTORY

Of all the big Cadillac sedans of the sixties, the elegant Fleetwood Brougham is the most beloved by enthusiasts, and the only one with any pretensions to collectibility. It was popular in its day, too, and handily outsold the conventional Sixty-Special, which was little more than an extended DeVille. One reason for the Brougham's appeal was that it was truly a reincarnation of the old Eldorado Brougham idea, with many standard luxury features and genuine class. Another was

that it carried the always-saleable Fleetwood nameplate. And a third was that it was once again distinctively different, with its 133-inch wheelbase. (Cadillac is tradition-minded. It started off the postwar years with a 133-inch Sixty-Special and came back to it twenty years later.)

The 1966-70 Fleetwood Brougham was only ostensibly a Sixty-Special; most often it was known by its body designation. Equipment was opulent: a padded vinyl roof with beaded edge molding, Brougham script on the upper rear roof quarters in case anyone

Brougham started out as a padded top option in 1965 on the Sixty-Special and returned in 1966 as a separate padded top model loaded with luxury features. (Bud Juneau)

Fleetwood sedans and Broughams shared front end design with other series. (Bud Juneau)

121

forgot, embroidered cloth or quality glove-soft leather interiors, illuminated picnic tables for the rear-seat passengers, carpeted footrests and adjustable reading lamps. Much of the trim was genuine walnut.

Starting in 1966, Brougham was a separate model. (Bud Juneau)

The difference in price between this posh toy and the standard Sixty-Special was only a couple hundred dollars, so it's no wonder the Brougham outstripped its linemate. Cadillac built 17,300 Fleetwood Broughams in 1969 and, coupled with the basic Sixty-Special sedan, it ran off close to 20,000 Sixty-Specials—a figure not seen since 1957. With this new model, Cadillac had found the priceless middle ground between the other-worldly Eldorado Brougham of 1957-58 and the underwhelming DeVille-like Sixty-Specials of the recent past. It was a good

Fleetwood series was identified by the Wreath & Crest. (Bud Juneau)

Cadillac's distinctive headlamp arrangement. (Bud Juneau)

Turn-signal indicators in the fenders were supposed to be in driver's line of sight. (Bud Juneau)

move, and it's been quite a hit for Cadillac in the years since.

IDENTIFICATION

Laurel wreath and crest on hood and trunk; "Fleetwood" in block letters on front fenders; heavy chrome rocker panel molding. Fleetwood Brougham has "Brougham" script on rear roof quarters; vinyl covered, padded roofs, much interior wood or wood-like trim.

PERFORMANCE AND UTILITY

The performance and utility of these cars matched those of the 1965-70 Calais and DeVille.

PROBLEM AREAS

In addition to the problems listed for the 1965-70 Calais and DeVille, which apply here, special Brougham trim is hard to find.

Individual letters have a look of elegance. (Bud Juneau)

Adjustable reading lamps first appeared in 1966 on the Broughams only. (Bud Juneau)

Driver can control all windows and vent panes, and can lock out all other buttons. (Bud Juneau)

Lavish wood door trim shown here on the 1966 Brougham, diminished to a thin veneer by 1969, and has been vinyl or plastic ever since. (Bud Juneau)

SUMMARY AND PROSPECTS

It's very difficult to predict a great future for a car this big and thirsty in our brave new world of the eighties. However, collectors insist that the Fleetwood Brougham stands head and shoulders above just about every other closed Cadillac of its era—and many would prefer one even to an Eldorado. But there's a definite division in their minds between the 1966-69 models and the post-1969 models, which is why this chapter ends in 1970.

Aside from the well-known driveability problems that beset big V-8s in the seventies, the Brougham was cheapened as the inevitable beancounters at Cadillac had their say. For example, the last of the real wood trim departed in 1969, and in its place came good old plastic. It wasn't really good wood, says collector Owen Hoyt, and personally he'd consider putting a good veneer over it (shudders from his colleagues, interviewed by Bud Juneau!)—but by gosh it was real wood-off-a-tree, and that's something. Stick to pre-seventies in your shopping.

VARIATIONS

Some Fleetwood Broughams saw limousine and livery service, and a few were specially ordered with unique trim. For example, in San Francisco a fleet of 1967s was painted jet black and had gray broadcloth upholstery and divider windows fitted. They were magnificent cars, and variants like them are well worth looking for.

1966-70 Sixty-Special	
ENGINE	
As per Chapter 28	
CHASSIS AND DRIVETRAIN	
As per Chapter 28	
GENERAL	
Wheelbase:	133.0 in.
Overall length:	228.5 in.
Track:	62.5 in. front and rear
Tire size:	1966-69: 9.00x15; 1970: L78x15
Weight:	4615-4835 lb.
PERFORMANCE	
As per Chapter 28	

1966 is considered by some collectors to be the Brougham high-point with illuminated fold-down trays, no-cost leather options, lavish wood trim, padded top, adjustable reading lamps and fold-down footrests. (Bud Juneau)

Illuminated fold-down trays were found on the 1966 and 1967 Broughams only. (Bud Juneau)

PRODUCTION	1966	1967	1968	1969	1970
Model 68069* four-door sedan	5,455	3,550	3,300	2,545	1,738
Model 68169** Fleetwood Brougham	13,630	12,750	15,300	17,300	16,913

* Designation changed to 68089 in 1970.
** Designation changed to 68189 in 1970.

The 1967 Brougham still had fold-down trays, footrests, and reading lamps, but lavish wood trim was dropped. Still, it is popular with collectors with its traditional Cadillac grille pattern and handsome good looks. (Bud Juneau)

The 1969 Sixty-Special sedan carried the Wreath & Crest down on the fender by the taillight. It shared the longer wheelbase with the Brougham, but lacked padded top, footrests and reading lamps. (Bud Juneau)

Eldorado
1967-70

★★★↙

HISTORY

This Eldorado was a revolutionary development for Cadillac, as important as the 1949 model. It was the first of the marque with front-wheel drive and an entirely new approach to Eldorado's marketplace. The technology wasn't new; Oldsmobile's Toronado had made its debut the year before. But the Eldo's styling was quite different from the Toronado's. It was the first time Bill Mitchell had applied his five-seat "personal car" theme to a Cadillac (his major past work in that field being the Buick Rivieras). It was one of the great shapes of the sixties, completely lacking rough spots, good looking from every angle, yet sufficiently "formal" to be consistent with Cadillac's current styling. (For a while management considered calling it La Salle instead of Eldorado, but dropped the idea after reading a book that called the La Salle Cadillac's "only failure.")

In addition to superb styling, the 1967 Eldorado was blessed with equally good engineering. What Cadillac had wanted was a large, luxurious car with all the traditional virtues allied to outstanding roadability. Cadillac teamed the 429 V-8 with a "split" transmission: The torque converter and

On the 1967, the traditional egg-crate grille was used. Outer sections of grille swung away when headlights were in use—they tended to be reliable.

1967 Eldo was clean and uncluttered at rear, with fenders split by slender, chrome and body-color bar.

With the DeVille convertible in the background, here's the splendid 1967 Eldorado, with front-wheel-drive and the best roadability anyone could remember in a Cadillac. Strongly recommended.

gearbox were separate from each other, linked by a chain drive and sprocket. The key was the chain, developed by Hydra-matic Division and Borg-Warner: unbreakable, flexible, light and not too costly to produce. The split transmission made the drivetrain quite compact.

The new front-wheel-drive Eldorado was not greatly changed until 1971, when it acquired a heavier, bulkier body and a companion convertible model. (At the same time, convertibles were dropped from the standard line.) The 1967-70 models were uniformly popular, with the 1968-70s selling around 24,000 each model year; the only reason the 1967 didn't do as well was that it started late in the year. In retrospect, this was one of the most historic Cadillacs of the postwar years, and intrinsically one of the most roadworthy and fun to drive.

IDENTIFICATION

Throughout, a formal, closed coupe with chiseled lines and a very long hood.

1967: Egg-crate grille with headlamps hidden by flanking egg-crates left and right. Parking lights mounted in bumper.

1968: Grillework unchanged but parking lamps shifted to extremities of front fenders.

1969: Finer-mesh grille and exposed headlamps. Halo-type vinyl roof. Rub rail strip along center of body sides. 8.2 Litre badge on left of grille, which was only slightly revised with more obvious horizontal bars.

Slotted wheel covers 1967-68, turbine types in 1969-70.

PERFORMANCE AND UTILITY

Front-wheel drive gave the Eldorado almost neutral handling characteristics. *Automobile Quarterly* Editor Don Vorderman wrote that, in cornering, the car displayed "mounting understeer when under full power, but this is easily neutralized by backing off the accelerator, at which time the tail will move but in the classic FWD tradition . . . It is doubtful that one owner in a thousand will drive the car this way, but it does speak volumes on how thoroughly Cadillac engineers have done their job."

With other Cadillacs, Eldorado shifted to the 472 V-8 in 1968, but in 1970 it acquired its own engine, stroked out to 500 cubic inches and producing 400 bhp. The largest V-8 Cadillac had produced, it was at once powerful and thirsty, and required leaded premium fuel.

A Cadillac that is fun to drive, in a way no predecessor had been, the Eldorado's pleasures are derived not only from front drive but from smaller-than-previous dimensions: The wheelbase, for example, is only 120 inches.

Roof design was formal, wheel openings full on 1967. Most collectors despise the lack of vent windows, but flow-through ventilation is efficient.

PROBLEM AREAS

Chain failure in the transmission is a common problem, as is U-joint failure. (According to John Bond, former publisher of *Road & Track,* any component that's expected to both drive and steer is going to give trouble.) The 1967 was the best version of the 429, the most highly developed, but compared to other Cadillac V-8 models this is not the best powerplant; the 1968-69 472 and 1970 500 are both much better. Rust is something to watch for, too.

SUMMARY AND PROSPECTS

Only the 1967 Eldorado has been named a Milestone thus far, but that the 1968-70 models will join it seems only a matter of time. Enginewise they were better cars. All four years are collectible, and their star ratings are in fact limited only by the fact that they all require leaded premium—and lots of it. These are very sound investments in original condition, which is the only way to buy them. Restorations are complicated, and probably not cost effective. Originals stand to appreciate rapidly in the future.

PRODUCTION	*1967*	*1968*
Model 69347		
coupe	17,930	24,528

	1969	*1970*
	23,333	28,842

The 1968 Eldo is just as desirable as the 1967. Parking lamps moved outboard, grillework was unchanged.

1967-70 Eldorado

ENGINE

Type: . . . . 8-cylinder 90° V-type, watercooled, cast iron block
and heads
Bore x stroke: . . . . 1967-69: 4.30x4.06 in.; 1970: 4.30x4.30 in.
Displacement: . . . . 1967-69: 472.0 ci; 1970: 500.0 ci
Valve operation: . . . . overhead, pushrod actuated
Compression ratio: 1967-69: 10.5:1; 1970: 10.0:1
Carburetion: . . . . 1967-69: Rochester Quadra-Jet #7028230; 1970:
Rochester Quadra-Jet #4MV
Bhp: . . . . 1967-69: 375 bhp at 4400 rpm; 1970: 400 bhp at 4400 rpm
(gross)

CHASSIS AND DRIVETRAIN

Transmission: . . . . . Turbo Hydra-matic longitudinally mounted with
transfer case
Final drive ratio: 3.21:1
Rear suspension: . . . . . single-leaf longitudinal semi-elliptic springs,
live axle
Front suspension: . . . independent via torsion bar and A-arms, tube
shocks
Frame: . . . . integral boxed perimeter

GENERAL

Wheelbase: . . . . 120.0 in.
Overall length: . . . . 221.0 in.
Track: . . . . 63.0 in. front, 63.5 in. rear
Tire size: 1967-69: 9.00x15; 1970: L78x15/D-75
Weight: . . . . 4500-4630 lb.

PERFORMANCE (1967)

Acceleration: . . . . 0-80: 15.3 seconds
Top speed: . . . . 125-130 mph
Fuel mileage: . . . . 12-14 mpg

Finer-mesh grille took some distinction from the car
in 1969. My guess is that the 1967-68s will eventually develop a slight lead in value on the 1969-70,
though all are essentially the same car.

In 1970, Cadillac built a record 28,842 Eldorados, restyled slightly with installed square grillework. One plus for the 1969-70 models is that they used the new 472 V-8, which was a better engine than the 429 of 1967-68.

Chapter 31

Fleetwood Seventy-Five 1968-76

★★ Fleetwood Seventy-Five 1968-76

HISTORY

Like the Sixty Special in this period, the famous Fleetwood Seventy-Five was putting in its last appearance as a truly monumental Cadillac. From 1968, Seventy-Fives received the new, larger 472 V-8, while dimensions remained unchanged at 149.8 inches wheelbase and 20 feet overall length. A complete restyle occurred for 1971, and like the Sixty Special, the Seventy-Five was fractionally larger than before. Its wheelbase was now 151.5 inches and it weighed 2 1/2 tons. The traditional long sedan and limousine were offered, along with a commercial chassis on a six-inch-longer wheelbase. Automatic Level Control, carpeted footrests, fixed-ratio power steering and Automatic Climate Control were standard. Twilight Sentinel became standard in 1975, dual front/rear Automatic Climate Control in 1976. Harking back to the days of semi-custom coachbuilt bodies, the rear roofline was available in several patterns, including fully closed, coach-window style, and with maximum glass area. Aft of the cowl, design changes during the period were mild and evolutionary, and there was never any change in body styles, which typically amounted to about 1,000 sedans, 1,000 limousines, and 2,000 commercial chassis.

IDENTIFICATION

1968: Obviously longer than other models; limousines have driver's compartment partition. Fine mesh grille; doors cut into roof, Fleetwood wreath and crest emblems, power front ventipanes, vertical headlamps.

1969: Horizontal headlamps with parking/cornering lights integrated into leading edge of front fenders.

1970: Minor facelift. Grille has 13 vertical blades sent against fine mesh.

1971: Restyled along lines of other 1971 Cadillacs. Several rear roof quarter designs were available.

1972: Horizontal grille blades, parking lamps between quad headlamps. Fleetwood lettering on front fenders. Side windows with rounded corners.

1973: Energy-absorbing bumpers combined with egg-crate style grille; wider spaced quad headlamps allowed much wider parking lights in between.

1974: New egg-crate grille with larger "egg-holes." Quad headlamps now mounted close together with parking lights outboard and wrapped around front fenders. Vertical chrome bumper ends with taillights built in. New curved instrument panel.

1975: Square headlamps. Cross-hatch pattern grille. New coach-style windows on rear roof quarters.

1976: Wreath and crest on deck (not "V" and crest as on junior models). Horizontal chrome trim on cornering lamps, large horizontal taillamps set into rear bumper.

SPECIFICATIONS

ENGINE
Type: .... 8-cylinder V-type, cast iron block
Bore x stroke:. ....1968-74: 4.30 x 4.06 in.;
....1975-76: 4.30 x 4.30 in.
Displacement: ....1968-74: 472.0 ci; 1975-76: 500.0 ci
Valve operation: ....overhead
Compression ratio: 1968-73: 10:1; 1974: 8.25:1; 1975-76: 8.5:1
Induction system: .... 4bbl carburetor; fuel injection optional, 1975-76
Bhp: .... 1968-74: 375 at 4400 rpm (gross), 220 (net); 1974: 205 at 4000 rpm (net); 1976: 190 at 3600 rpm, 215 at 3600 rpm (fuel injection)

CHASSIS AND DRIVETRAIN
Transmission: .... Turbo Hydra-matic
Front suspension: .... independent, coil springs, tube shocks
Rear suspension: .... live axle, coil springs, tube shocks
Frame: .... full perimeter

GENERAL
Wheelbase: ....1968-70: 149.8 in.; 1971-75: 151.5 in.
Overall length:.. 245-253 in.
Overall width: .... 80.0 in.
Tire size: L78x15
Weight: .... 5300-5900 lbs.

PERFORMANCE
Acceleration: .... 0-60: 15 seconds
Top speed: .... 110 mph
Fuel mileage: .... 10-15 mpg

PERFORMANCE AND UTILITY

Like all Seventy-Fives, these are massive automobiles and formidable to navigate in tight quarters unless you are a professional chauffeur trained to the task. They are not relatively expensive to buy but are costly to run and live with, impossible to restore and brutes to service. Still, they are among the most impressive cars the American industry has produced, and they have their partisans.

PROBLEM AREAS

Considerable technical complexity attends all Fleetwood Seventy-Fives of this period. In this writer's day a kid was expected to be able to take apart an M.G. and put it back together again, restored, with little more than a shop manual. Not even genius kids would attempt that with a Fleetwood limousine. Special trim pieces are impossible to find as replacement items; access to a parts car would be a big help.

SUMMARY AND PROSPECTS

Remarkably, Seventy-Five list prices didn't exceed $30,000 until 1983, and today they are probably the best bargains in the executive car class—whether or not this a plus or minus for collectors we should not, perhaps, speculate.

PRODUCTION

	1968	1969	1970	1971	1972	1973	1974	1975	1976
Sedan	805	880	876	752	955	1,043	895	876	981
Limousine	995	1,156	1,240	848	960	1,017	1,005	795	834
Chassis	2,413	2,550	2,506	2,014	2,462	2,212	2,265	1,329	1,509

Chapter 32

Calais, DeVille 1971-76

★ Calais, DeVille 1971-76

HISTORY

Despite a thorough restyle in 1971, the model hierarchy was left intact. But since the Eldorado had now gained a convertible body style, the DeVille convertible was dropped—a significant loss to collectors. Calais remained the least expensive model, though it wasn't much cheaper than the DeVille, which differed only in its rather more elaborate trim and upholstery. Calais always took the smaller share of sales. These big cars on the General Motors C-body continued to dominate Cadillac's output until the arrival of the Seville in 1975. By 1972 the Calais, however, was almost superfluous, accounting for fewer than 8,000 units, while the DeVille hardtops (coupe and sedan) continued as Cadillac's breadwinners, selling nearly 200,000 between them. The country was prosperous, and the typical Cadillac buyer preferred to pay a little extra for the up-market model. In 1973 Cadillac pro-

The 1974 Cadillac Sedan de Ville represented the bulk of four-door Cadillac sales. Long and wide, it packed the standard 472 cid V-8, but emission controls reduced horsepower to 205 (net) this year from 220 the year before.

duced another record: over 300,000 units, the first time this mark had been topped in Division history. Most of these were De-Villes, which, with the Calais, had a minor facelift. But they were chiefly recognizable by their enormous, clumsy looking energy-absorbing bumpers, to which grilles were now directly attached. Collectors tend to consider the crash-bumper a negative factor when compared to 1971-72 models. Features of the 1974 models included new lighting designs, fixed rectangular quarter windows for coupes, lower profiles and rear chrome bumper ends with built-in taillights. Changes were moderate in 1975-76, mainly centering around new colors and materials for the interior and distinguishing front end styling.

IDENTIFICATION

1971: Hidden windshield wipers. Cadillac crest on center front hood. New turn repeater lamps atop front fenders. Horizontal back-up lamps set into rear bumper. Nameplates identify Calais and DeVille.

1972: Horizontal grille blades, parking lights between quad headlamps

1973: Energy-absorbing bumpers combined with egg-crate style grille; wider spaced quad headlamps allowed much wider parking lights in between.

1974: New egg-crate grille with larger "egg-holes." Quad headlamps now mounted close together with parking lights outboard and wrapped around front fenders.

This 1975 Calais four-door sedan is an extremely rare car. Only 2,500 were built, against another handful (5,800) of the Calais coupe. Collectibility has not so far been enhanced by scarcity, as enthusiasts don't distinguish much between Calais and the more popular, up-market DeVille.

Vertical chrome bumper ends with taillights built in. New curved instrument panel.

1975: Square headlamps. Cross-hatch pattern grille. New coach-style windows on rear roof quarters.

1976: Horizontal chrome trim on cornering lamps, large horizontal taillamps set into rear bumper. "V" and crest on decklids.

PERFORMANCE AND UTILITY

These are expensive cars to own, run and maintain, but they repay their partisans with opulent size and a pillowy ride, the like of which we haven't really seen since. Drivability improved as the decade wore on and engineers began to master the efficient compliance with pollution and safety regulations. Fuel mileage was also better. EPA ratings for the 1976 DeVille were 12 city and 16 highway; by really trying, some owners say they can nurse 20 mpg on a highway trip. These were quality cars which perhaps missed the mark for the new crop of buyers with different automotive perspectives, but they still offered good value for money in prestige and quality for those who valued size and comfort.

PROBLEM AREAS

Cadillac reliability during this period was good, but collectors should be aware that these are complicated machines, likely to cost a lot to fix when any one of the myriad of gadgets and accessories goes wrong, not to mention fuel injection on the later models. The carburetor versions are far more amenable to back-yard mechanics. Body and trim parts are increasingly scarce, and a major restoration on these models is not recommended—instead, buy the best condition car you can find, even at a price, because it will be cheaper in the long run.

SUMMARY AND PROSPECTS

Very solid, well built cars, these Cadillacs have not yet been collected widely, and their potential appreciation value is presently low, but many are around to choose from. Among the 1974-76 models, look for the special trim packages: Coupe DeVille d'Elegance (velour upholstery, both models) and Cabriolet (landau type rear roof treatment) and the Coupe de Ville (a Cabriolet with power sun roof). The 1976 d'Elegance was especially different, with standard opera windows (optional on other coupes), special see-through hood ornament and striping on hood and doors, etc. Another interesting point about these Cadillacs is that the hardtop coupe was usually produced in far greater quantity than the four-door sedan, which makes the latter more desirable than usual, but probably still not as valuable as the hardtop coupe. Finally, a historical note: these were the last of the truly mammoth Cadillacs, and the 1976 models, being "last of the last," appeal to the collector instinct for historical reasons.

The 1976 Cadillac sedan models, Calais (shown here) and Sedan de Ville, were the last before extensive downsizing set in. Subtly refined in appearance from 1975, they offered optional wire wheel discs, including one with black center hub area (Calais) similar to the Eldorado. Vinyl roofs, in eleven colors, were finished in an elk grain pattern. Only 1,700 Calais sedans were built compared to over 67,000 Sedan de Villes.

PRODUCTION

Calais	1971	1972	1973	1974	1975	1976
hardtop sedan	3,569	3,875	3,798	2,324	2,500	1,700
hardtop coupe	3,360	3,900	4,275	4,559	5,800	4,500

PRODUCTION

DeVille	1971	1972	1973	1974	1975	1976
hardtop sedan	69,345	99,531	103,394	60,419	63,352	67,677
hardtop coupe	66,081	95,280	112,849	112,201	110,218	114,482

SPECIFICATIONS

ENGINE
Type: .... 8-cylinder V-type, cast iron block
Bore x stroke: 1971-74: 4.30 x 4.06 in.; 1975-76: 4.30 x 4.30 in.
Displacement: ....1971-74: 472.0 ci; 1975-76: 500.0 ci
Valve operation: ....overhead
Compression ratio: 1971-73: 10:1; 1974: 8.25:1; 1975-76: 8.5:1
Induction system: .... 4bbl carburetor; fuel injection optional 1975-76
Bhp: .... 1971-74: 375 at 4400 rpm (gross), 220 (net); 1975: 205 at 4000 rpm (net); 1976: 190 at 3600 rpm, 215 at 3600 rpm (fuel injection)

CHASSIS AND DRIVETRAIN
Transmission: .... 3spd Turbo Hydra-matic
Front suspension: ...... independent, coil springs, tube shocks
Rear suspension: .... live axle, coil springs, tube shocks
Frame: .... full perimeter

GENERAL
Wheelbase: ....130.0 in.
Overall length: .... 225.8 in.
Overall width: .... 80.0 in.
Tire size: L78x15
Weight: .... 4600-4800 lbs.

PERFORMANCE
Acceleration: .... 0-60: 12 seconds
Top speed: .... 120 mph
Fuel mileage: .... 12-17 mpg

Chapter 33

Sixty Special Fleetwood Brougham, 1971-76

★★ Sixty Special Fleetwood Brougham, 1971-76

HISTORY

For 1971 the two previous owner-driver Fleetwoods—Brougham and Sixty Special—were merged into a single "Sixty Special Brougham," and that designation lasted through 1976. The 1971 through 1976 generation of Cadillac's respected, long-wheelbase model marked a temporary end to the name, though it would surface again on a limited production Fleetwood in 1987. Remarkably, the Sixty Special concept had changed little since the early postwar years, when a long sedan on a 133-inch wheelbase had existed to fill the needs of those who wanted extra space and the panache of the Fleetwood name. In some years the extra inches had gone into the trunk compartment rather than the passenger area, but Sixty Specials in the 1970s used the space to provide legroom. With the massive downsizing of 1977, the "Fleetwood Brougham" name passed to a standard-wheelbase Cadillac, and the owner-driver Sixty Special was dropped.

Everything Cadillac could throw in was standard on Sixty Special Fleetwood Broughams, including automatic level control, reading lamps, padded vinyl roof and separately adjustable front seat halves ("Dual Comfort"). Model year changes were restricted to detail styling modifications; in 1972 horsepower began to be expressed in

Over 15,000 Sixty Special Broughams were sold in 1971, with "everything standard" and a conservative, formal look, enhanced by the blind rear roof corners, slim coachlights behind the rear door windows, and squared-off grille.

Parking lamps, carried in front bumpers on the 1971 Broughams, moved to between the quad head-lamps on the '72s. Aside from that, there was nothing to distinguish the '72 model—even the wheel cover design remained the same.

net rather than gross figures. When the Sixty Special was retired in 1976, it could look back 37 years—an impressive run for a model which had always been an important part of the line. During this final period it sold between 15,000 and 25,000 copies per year, and was always profitable.

IDENTIFICATION

1971: Fleetwood name in block letters on front fenders; padded vinyl top; doors cut into roof limousine-style. Thick "B" pillar.

1972: Unique four side windows with rounded corners; parking lamps moved to between the quad headlamps.

1973: Should be equipped with carpeted rear compartment footrests. Energy-absorbing bumpers combined with egg-crate style grille; wider spaced quad headlamps allowed much wider parking lights in between.

1974: New egg-crate grille with larger "egg-holes." Quad headlamps now mounted close together with parking lights outboard and wrapped around front fenders. Vertical chrome bumper ends with taillights built in. New curved instrument panel.

1975: Square headlamps. Cross-hatch pattern grille. New coach-style windows on rear roof quarters.

1976: Wreath and crest on deck (not "V" and crest as on junior models.) Horizontal chrome trim on cornering lamps, large horizontal taillamps set into rear bumper.

PERFORMANCE AND UTILITY

Fast for its size, extremely easy to drive but bulky to navigate in tight quarters, the luxurious Sixty Special Brougham is everything you'd expect a semi-limousine to be. It is hardly a vehicle you would enter in a gymkhana, but few cars in the luxury field could match its spaciousness and refinement. Expect dreadful gas mileage, and a scarcity of body and trim parts, especially those unique to the Brougham. Cadillac took pains to provide quality; the tight, solid way everything fits and works together is indicative that they succeeded.

PROBLEM AREAS

Cadillac reliability during this period was good, but collectors should be aware that these are complicated machines, likely to cost a lot to fix when any one of the myriad

New wheelcovers and changes to bumpers to comply with crash protection requirements, marked the 1973 Sixty Special Brougham. The black bumper inserts front and rear helped meet government mandates. Original equipment whitewalls were ultra-slim. Basic body styling was unchanged, but note that the rear edge of the front door has been extended, eliminating the filler between the two doors.

Parking lights moved outboard for 1974, when they merged with the cornering lights, leaving the quad headlamps very close together. Wheelcovers regained the turbine blade look. Crash-bumpers were still massive, though lighter colored inserts gave them a less ponderous appearance.

SPECIFICATIONS

ENGINE
Type: .... 8-cylinder V-type, cast iron block
Bore x stroke: 1971-74: 4.30 x 4.06 in.; 1975-76: 4.30 x 4.30 in.
Displacement: ....1971-74: 472.0 ci; 1975-76: 500.0 ci
Valve operation: ....overhead
Compression ratio: 1971-73: 10:1; 1974: 8.25:1; 1975-76: 8.5:1
Induction system: .... 4bbl carburetor; fuel injection optional
    1975-76
Bhp: .... 1971-74: 375 at 4400 rpm (gross), 220 (net);
    1975: 205 at 4000 rpm (net);.1976: 190 at 3600 rpm, 215
    at 3600 rpm (fuel injection)

CHASSIS AND DRIVETRAIN
Transmission: .... 3spd Turbo Hydra-matic
Front suspension: ...... independent, coil springs, tube shocks
Rear suspension: .... live axle, coil springs, tube shocks
Frame: .... full perimeter

GENERAL
Wheelbase: ....133.0 in.
Overall length:...229-231 in.
Overall width: ....80.0 in.
Tire size: L78x15
Weight: .... 4800-5200 lbs.

PERFORMANCE
Acceleration: ....0-60: 13 seconds
Top speed: ....120 mph
Fuel mileage: ....11-16 mpg

of gadgets and accessories goes wrong, including fuel injection on the later models. The carburetor versions are far more amenable to back-yard mechanics. Body and trim parts are increasingly scarce, and a major restoration is not recommended. Instead, buy the best example you can find, because it will be cheaper in the long run.

SUMMARY AND PROSPECTS

In 1973-76, look for the special "Brougham d'Elegance" trim option, consisting of an ultra-posh interior with reading lamps and other niceties. One step up in 1974 was the "Fleetwood Talisman," with velour or leather upholstered armchair seating for four, separated by upholstered consoles containing writing sets and vanities. Broughams are still not hard to find, and a nice one could be a good investment, but avoid rough examples. The scarcest one is the 1971, but the 1976, being last of a long-running model and the most refined, is the best buy.

PRODUCTION	1971	1972	1973	1974	1975	1976
	15,200	20,750	24,800	18,250	18,755	24,500

The 1975 Sixty Special Brougham typifies the distinctive Fleetwood Brougham design and decor. The elegance of the Brougham was enhanced this year by wider whitewall tires, which were also steel-belted radials. "Brougham" script next to narrow vertical opera window on formal rear roof quarters also help visually identify the Sixty Special from the DeVille/Calais lines.

Chapter 34

Eldorado 1971-78

★★ convertible
★ coupe

HISTORY

The second generation of the front-wheel-drive land cruiser coupes is not as much fun to look at and less entertaining to drive, but still unique for a Cadillac—or for anything else. Offered throughout this period as a coupe (with vinyl top and narrow, oblong opera windows) or as a convertible, the latter being Cadillac's last production convertible until recently. All cars continued to use the 500 cid V-8, but tighter emissions limits caused rapid detuning; by 1975 the Eldo was rated (in net horsepower) at only 190 bhp. Existence of the convertible model (and its absence in the other lines) helped sales, and Eldorados soon accounted for a lucrative 40,000 sales per year.

In 1972, the Custom Cabriolet option arrived: electric sunroof with elk-grain vinyl roof aft of the opening and "halo" molding. An old Eldo feature adorned the 1972 convertible in the form of a hardtop boot for open driving. Heavier styling in 1973, but sales just kept increasing, and an Eldo convertible paced the Indianapolis 500. Electronic fuel injection was an option for 1975,

The 1971, with pinched waist, was the first new-generation Eldorado.

when Cadillac also introduced the Astro-roof, a tinted panel for the power sunroof, complete with auxiliary sunshade (a conventional metal slider was also available).

Cadillac announced that there would be no more convertibles after the 1976 Eldorados, and decided in advance to retain the last one for historic purposes. The final 200 were all produced in the exact image of that grand finale. Each was painted white with a white top, white-painted wheel covers and white upholstery, and a special dash plaque attested to its being the end of the run. (However, they were not the last, for no sooner had Chrysler returned a ragtop to its line via a special builder than Cadillac and others chimed in during 1983.)

Amply endowed with all the power options, including huge varieties of sound and comfort equipment, the 1971-76 Eldorados were probably the most opulent Cadillacs ever produced. They lasted in this form until 1979, when the front-wheel-drive car was extensively downsized, and they would never be this big again.

IDENTIFICATION

1971: "Pinched" waist trailing a dummy vertical scoop just aft of doors as on Cadillacs of the fifties. Exposed quad headlamps and parking lights in fender ends.

1972: More vertically textured grille, bearing Cadillac script on left. Eldorado script above front fender cornering lights. 8.2 Litre on front fenders.

1973: Back to the big egg-crate grille. Massive bumpers with rubber bump inserts.

1974: Same approach but a fine-mesh grille again. (Why didn't they just leave it alone?)

1975: Much squarer grille with square egg-crates and square quad headlamps.

1976: Grille higher than the flanking lights.

1977: Grille back to headlamp level, but a

1972 Eldorado received fender script nameplate, wider bars for grille.

broad piece of brightmetal affixed to hood just overhead.

1978: Larger-mesh egg-crate grille.

PERFORMANCE AND UTILITY

Though up six inches in wheelbase during this period, the Eldorado was not any longer; it remained at 222 inches, the overhang at both ends having been shortened. Nevertheless, it was quite a handful to drive compared to the 1967-70 generation, and far more of a traditional Cadillac in this respect.

PROBLEM AREAS

Driveability problems caused by choking emission controls make this one of the less satisfying Cadillacs to own. On the plus side, it'll run on unleaded gas. Its fit and finish are generally poorer than in 1967-70, though it has improved rust resistance. It is very expensive to restore.

SUMMARY AND PROSPECTS

The most ridiculous lawsuit since the monkey trial cropped up lately, when a couple of lawyers filed a class action suit against Cadillac. Reason? The Division had "promised" that the 1976 Eldo would be its last convertible, and here it was making them again, or at least allowing someone else to

Neat way to handle 1973 Eldorado rear marker light was to make it a badge.

Trim was shuffled again for 1974 Eldos, nobody knew why.

make them. The lawyers were part of a large group of people who bought 1976 Eldo "last" convertibles as an investment.

Very rarely do "made-to-order collectibles" really become collectible, and the people who buy such things as a 1976 Cadillac "collectors edition" are just proof that Barnum was right after all. Most often, collectible cars happen by accident. For instance, Cadillac built 14,000 ragtop Eldos for 1976—over 5,000 more than in 1975—because it had just 14,000 convertible soft top mechanisms available. Thus the 1975 is really a lot scarcer than the 1976, purely by manufacturer plan. Fourteen thousand is a lot of cars, and the 200 specially trimmed "last" models just weren't distinctive enough to warrant much of a fuss. Nevertheless, no sooner were they announced than people started paying happy dealers well above sticker prices (then about $12,000) to own one, and dealers who had stocked up against the expected onslaught of suckers happily obliged. Ignorant "money" magazines and even the National Auto Dealers Association *Used Car Guide* touted prices for these cars that were well above the 1975 price, as much as eight years after they were built. The fact is that a 1976 Eldorado is worth no more than a 1975, unless it's one of the last 200, in which case add a thousand dollars.

Wait a minute, prospective buyer of a 1976 "last convertible!" Let me give you a few facts: (1) It wasn't the last convertible. Even as Cadillac celebrated The End, AMC was happily turning out removable hardtop Jeeps and, as we now know, the ragtop made a comeback just a few years later. (2) Even if it was, it's little different and less scarce than the 1975 version. (3) People paid as much as thirty grand for one at a time when the truly collectible Eldorado Brougham was just working back to its original list price. Today the Eldo Brougham is worth up to $25,000, while the 1976 Eldorado convertible is pegged at around $10,000 in grade-A condition. (4) It's very hard to have an even chance suing General Motors!

Squarer grille and quad headlamps were featured on 1975 Eldorados.

PRODUCTION	1971	1972	1973	1974
Model 69347				
coupe	20,568	32,099	42,136	32,812
Model 69367				
convertible	6,800	7,975	9,315	7,600
	1975	1976	1977	1978
Model 69347				
coupe	35,802	35,184	47,344	46,816
Model 69367				
convertible	8,950	14,000	—	—

More detail alterations on the 1976, with body-color
wheel covers adding to the Eldorado's clean looks.

Opera windows had reached popular vogue by
1977 Eldorados.

SPECIAL MODELS

The Custom Cabriolet option of 1972 and later adds perhaps $1,000 to the value of an Eldorado, but should not be considered vital when shopping for one. Aftermarket or dealer conversions, like Superfly or El Doral models, have thus far been slugs on the collector car market, and deservedly.

The Custom Biarritz was first offered late in the 1976 model year and continued on 1977-78 Eldorados. This trim option proved popular and is not rare, but is valued by late-Eldo collectors. Included were thick padding on the rear part of the roof, limo-like backlight, coach lamps, special identification, chrome molding along the fenderline and Sierra-grain pillow-soft leather seats. Contrary to some beliefs, the Astro-roof or sunroof was not standard, but optional.

The Custom Biarritz Classic was an extension of the above concept for 1978, featuring special and gaudy two-tone paintwork. Generally, Biarritz models are worth more than Eldorado's stock examples, but not that much more. There really hasn't been a strong collector movement toward these cars yet, and there may never be. The best advice I can offer is to consider the first-generation 1967-70 models, which are definitely collectible and stand to appreciate in the years ahead.

1971-78 Eldorado
ENGINE

Type: . . . . 8-cylinder 90° V-type, watercooled, cast iron block and heads
Bore x stroke: . . . . . . 1971-76: 4.30x4.30 in.; 1977-78: 4.08x4.06 in.
Displacement: . . . . 1971-76: 500.0 ci; 1977-78: 425 ci
Valve operation: . . . . overhead, pushrod actuated
Compression ratio: 1971: 9.0:1; 1972-73: 8.5:1; 1974-78: 8.25:1
Carburetion: . . . . Rochester 4bbl
Bhp: . . . . . . 1971-72: 365 bhp at 4400 rpm (gross); 1973: 235 bhp at 4400 rpm (net); 1974: 210 bhp at 4400 rpm; 1975-76: 190 bhp at 4400 rpm; 1977-78: 180 bhp at 4400 rpm (all 1974-78 figures net bhp)

CHASSIS AND DRIVETRAIN

As per Chapter 30

GENERAL

Wheelbase: . . . . 126.3 in.
Overall length: . . . . 1971-73: 223 in.; 1974-78: 225 in.
Track: . . . . 63.0 in. front, 63.5 in. rear
Tire size: 1971-74: L78x15; 1975-78: LR78x15
Weight: . . . . 4675-5167 lb.

PERFORMANCE

Acceleration . . . . 0-80: 19.0 seconds
Top speed: . . . . 115-120 mph
Fuel mileage: . . . . 10-13 mpg

Last of a breed and last of the jumbo Eldorados, the 1978 model will probably have curiosity value for that reason. Upkeep is high, though.

Chapter 35

Seville
1975-79

★★★ **Elegante**
★★★ **San Remo (1978-79)**
★★ **Seville (1975-79)**
★★ **gasoline engine**
★ **diesel engine (1978-79)**

HISTORY

LaSalle would have been a perfect name for this new and pioneering "international-size" Cadillac, but once again management people shied away from a name they associated with failure. Ultimately they reached back twenty years and revived a name Cadillac had once shared with DeSoto: Seville. It

The new, small Cadillac has already built quite a favorable reputation with collectors of old, large models, and enjoys increasing value ten years after it was first built. Look for clean, low-mileage ones.

was an immediate hit. Although it rode the shortest wheelbase in sixty-five years, the Seville appealed to the needs of the times; after a late introduction it sold in increasing numbers, around 50,000 per year. True, it was based on something eminently non-Cadillac (wags called them Avons—Nova spelled backward). Until 1977 it wasn't available with unpadded tops because it was cheaper to cover the cobbled Nova roofwork with vinyl than to finish it smoothly.

But the Seville was a really nice car, something over which Cadillac had taken pains. Styling was a bit truncated and square, but the taut, all-of-a-piece looks were viewed well. The 5.7 liter Olds-designed V-8 with electronic fuel injection gave 0-60 in eleven seconds and easy, low-revving cruising. The Seville rode as well as any recent Cadillac, and it handled better than all of them. It wouldn't quite fly over rutted concrete like a 450SE Mercedes, but it cost less than half as much. It was a whole new approach to the American concepts of luxury motoring, and in Cadillac's wake—as usual—all its rivals quickly followed.

The package was improved with four-wheel disc brakes in 1977, and in 1978 a diesel engine option was announced, along with a sophisticated electronic trip computer. The 1979s, last of this generation, had retuned suspensions and new body mounts,

SEVILLE INSTRUMENT PANEL

SEVILLE LUGGAGE COMPARTMENT

SEVILLE DOOR CONTROL PANELS

SEVILLE LIGHTING ARRANGEMENT

Details of the 1975 Seville, which was a spring introduction that year. Controls and fitments were posh and sensible, designed for efficiency.

along with a host of special-trim sub-models.

In all, Seville lasted five model years, quite a run for a postwar Cadillac; its replacement ran even longer. Times, they were a-changing, and in the downsized world of the late seventies, the Standard of the World was still the Standard.

IDENTIFICATION

Virtually no changes between 1975 and 1976 models; the 1976 was a continuation of the very limited 1975 model run.

1977: Fine-mesh grille with mainly vertical emphasis. Optional wire wheel covers and four-wheel disc brakes.

1978: Engraved taillight emblems. Rear accent striping. Optional opera lights, chrome wire wheels, diesel engine.

1979: Finer-mesh grille. Nameplate on upper left grille instead of upper right as in 1978.

PERFORMANCE AND UTILITY

This car gave excellent performance and fuel mileage unprecedented in the Cadillac class (20 mpg driven very carefully over the open road) in a car that rode and handled like something from Europe. It took every road surface in stride and handled with assurance (some roll, but no wallowing). Compared to the Mercedes, against which it was sold, the braking was as good (from 1977 on), the steering a bit slower and a tad less precise. It had plenty of room and excellent ergonomics inside.

The Europeans still considered it a shade gauche, but there was just as much chrome on their Mercedes-Benz, and they had to recognize Cadillac's tremendous international sales appeal for the first time in living memory. For the collector in search of daily transportation with some appreciation potential, the Seville should be attractive.

PROBLEM AREAS

Early fuel injection inclined to hard cold-starts, hesitation and even catching fire—it should be carefully tended by experts. Frames are said to be weak: According to one collector, "If you unload one off a ship and drop it just a bit hard, it's had it." The ohv V-8 was a fine engine, but the diesel (1978-79 option) left much to be desired. It had a reputation for short life (quite the contrary of traditional diesels)—some say because it was designed from a conventional engine. It has plenty of performance for a diesel, but is not recommended.

The 1976 Seville saw no alterations from successful 1975 intro package.

Here's a Seville without the vinyl top. Such cars were uncommon, especially in the earlier years (this is a 1977 model), but collectors gravitate toward their cleaner lines. Definitely worth looking for.

More of the same, plus engraved taillamp lenses: Seville for 1978.

SUMMARY AND PROSPECTS

Most Cadillacs of the seventies are too young to be considered by collectors, but the Seville is a definite exception. "Let's face it," says one collector, "the tank is out. Super leaded gas is a problem on any Cadillac from 1957 to 1970. The Seville is the right size, it's a pleasure to drive under modern conditions. And it looks like a Cadillac, despite its size." I'd say that makes it a car to look for.

Collectors seem to prefer the cleaner-looking Sevilles without padded tops (1977 and beyond). One, a devotee of Packards and other fine Classics, held out on his order

Last year for first-generation Seville again saw only evolutionary changes and trim shuffles.

until a reluctant dealer found him one. It's not hard to visualize this car—at least fine original examples of it—as a collector item years from now. It has history, style, performance and handling to spare—even more than the contemporary Eldorados.

PRODUCTION

	1975	1976	1977	1978	1979
Model 6KS69 four-door sedan	16,355	43,772	45,060	56,985	53,487

SPECIAL MODELS

The following variations on the Seville theme are worth looking out for. Built in limited quantities, they're a cut above the norm. Specials like these have traditionally retained strong collector appeal.

The Seville Elegante (1978) featured distinctive two-tone exterior paintwork, the second color starting just above the beltline, with a painted roof. There were brushed, chrome-plated side moldings where the colors met, true wire wheels (chrome plated), perforated leather seats and a center console. Typical Elegantes were Sable black over Platinum; they were also done in Saddle Firemist combined with Ruido brown. Only 5,000 were built.

The Elegante continued in 1979 as a $2,700 option. Many specials were built by conversion firms, notably the San Remo convertible—a beautiful, workmanlike conversion that looked as if Cadillac had built it. Unlike most conversions, this one is definitely collectible.

1975-79 Seville

ENGINE
Type: . . . . 8-cylinder 90° V-type, watercooled, cast iron block and heads; diesel version optional 1978-79
Bore x stroke: . . . . 4.06x3.39 in.
Displacement: . . . . 350.0 ci
Valve operation: . . . . overhead, pushrod actuated
Compression ratio: 8.0:1
Induction system: . . . . electronic fuel injection
Bhp: . . . . 1975-77: 180 bhp at 4400 rpm; 1978-79: 170 bhp at 4400 rpm; diesel engine 120-125 bhp (all figures net)

CHASSIS AND DRIVETRAIN
Transmission: . . . . Turbo Hydra-matic
Final drive ratio: 2.56:1
Rear suspension: . . . . . . self-leveling, live axle, semi-elliptic springs, tube shocks
Front suspension: . . independent, A-arms, coil springs, tube shocks, sway bar
Frame: . . . . unit body and chassis assembly with sub-frames

GENERAL
Wheelbase: . . . . 113.9 in.
Overall length: . . . . 204.0 in.
Track: . . . . 61.3 in. front, 59.0 in. rear
Tire size: GR78-15
Weight: . . . . 4180-4230 lb.

PERFORMANCE (1975-76)
Acceleration: . . . . 0-60: 11.5 seconds; 0-80: 22.7 seconds
Top speed: . . . . 115 mph
Fuel mileage: . . . . 15-17 mpg

DeVille, Fleetwood Limousine, 1977-84 Fleetwood Brougham, 1977-86 Brougham, 1987-92 Fleetwood, 1993

★★ DeVille, Fleetwood Limousine, 1977-84
★★ Fleetwood Bougham, 1977-86
★★ Brougham, 1987-92
★★★ Fleetwood, 1993

HISTORY

Dramatically shortened and lightened, the 1977 Coupe and Sedan DeVille were 221 inches long, ten inches shorter than in 1976 and about 1000 pounds lighter. The Fleetwood Brougham, now a deluxe DeVille with standard-length wheelbase, shrank even more. The Fleetwood Limousine (no longer called Seventy-five) was also downsized, and offered in two body styles: sedan and formal sedan. The 425 cid powerplant was new, and in keeping with the lighter bodies, smaller and less powerful. The model lineup was unchanged until 1980, when the long-

wheelbase formal was dropped and a coupe version of the Fleetwood Brougham added. The latter reestablished the old Sixty-one/Sixty-two, Calais/DeVille relationship of two popular lines with two-and four-door models, differing in trim and equipment. Less traditional was the offering, by mid-model-year, of a V-6 engine option, a 250 ci powerplant built by Buick. In 1981 Cadillac replaced the 425 (7 liter) V-8 with a 368 (6 liter), and offered an Oldsmobile 5.7 liter Diesel as an option. A squarer roofline allowed a few extra inches of passenger space. For 1982 Cadillac introduced another new engine, a fuel-injected 4.1 liter (250 ci) V-8 as standard for all models except the

Following a dramatic diet, the new 1977 Fleetwood Brougham (d'Elegance trim package shown here) lost 900 pounds in the process of shifting from 1976's 133-inch wheelbase to the standard 121.5-inch de Ville platform. It still looked exactly like a Cadillac, and customers responded, buying 28,000 copies, a healthy increase from the previous year.

The desirable "Phaeton" version of the Coupe de Ville offered a convertible-life roof covering and special interior touches; wire wheels were a nice touch. This is a 1979 model.

Cimarron and big limousines. This replaced the troublesome 6-liter 368 (V-8-6-4) engine, but the Buick V-6, which was optional through 1982, was less complicated and offered about the same performance.

After 1984 the Fleetwood Brougham was the only rear-wheel-drive Cadillac left in the line. It has gone through two confusing nomenclature changes, being referred to only as the "Brougham" for 1987-92, returning as the "Fleetwood" for 1993. Every year the road test magazines would say its days were numbered, but the following year it would be back, sustained by a substantial number of customers who still wanted Cadillacs of the old school. A drop in gasoline prices actually caused demand for it to rise by 30 percent during 1986, causing Cadillac to triple production and limit annual changes to details only. It was the last Cadillac to receive airbag passive restraints.

The only 1985 change was a Federally mandated high-mount center rear stop lamp; for 1987 a 5000-pound trailer-towing option was added. New standard features for 1988 were a tilt/telescoping steering wheel, heavy-duty battery, P225/75R15 self-sealing tires and 25-gallon fuel tank; in 1989 the list included cruise control and intermittent wipers. Responding to complaints of poor performance, Cadillac offered a 5.7 liter V-8 with 175 hp as an option in 1990, the year anti-lock brakes became standard. With EPA ratings of 14 mpg city, the 5.7-liter carried an $850 gas-guzzler tax. Yet it was just what Brougham buyers wanted, and 60 percent of the cars carried it; for 1991 the 5.7 gained 10 horsepower but the guzzler tax dropped to $550; the larger engine became standard in 1992. The Brougham (or "Fleetwood" as it was called for 1993) has continued to receive useful improvements in recent years. For 1991, the suspension was tauter than before, resulting in better ride control, and the variable-assist steering gave more feel at highway speeds.

IDENTIFICATION

1977: Oblong headlamps at extremities of body; short egg-crate grille with pattern repeated on underpart of front bumper. Front seatbelt retractors hidden in "B" pillars for first time.

1978: Bold horizontal cross-hatch grille. Vertical taillights in bumper ends with three-dimensional crest insignia. Aluminum hoods on many Broughams and all California cars. Optional Dunlop chrome wire wheels; signal seeking radios standard.

Standard-bearers for Cadillac in 1979, the Sedan (shown here) and Coupe de Ville accounted for well over 200,000 sales. This model year was marked by the fine-mesh grille with the grille theme repeated in the center part of the front bumper.

Crisp styling marked the Fleetwood Brougham in the early eighties. A forward-peaked grille and the controversial V-8-6-4 were used in 1981, but styling remained evolutionary, Cadillac having decided to avoid dramatic changes.

The 1983 Sedan de Ville, showing the narrow vertical-format grille bars segmented in three rows, flanked by oversquare headlamp/parking lamp combinations and outboard cornering lights.

1979. Cadillac script on upper righthand grille bar. Complicated cross-hatch grille repeated in twin openings under bumper. Seatbelt chimes.

1980: Streamlined stand-alone grille composed of narrow vertical bars; flush-mount headlamps above new amber horizontal parking/turn signal lamps.

1981: Standard "modulated displacement" V-8-6-4 engine or Olds Diesel. New forward peaked grille with wide header bar.

1982: New grille made up of vertical bars, sectioned by two horizontal bars, Cadillac script at righthand side of upper grille header.

1983: Narrow vertical grille bars separated in three rows; Cadillac script at side of grille.

1984: Bodyside moldings color keyed to body finish; goldtone Cadillac wing crests in taillamp lenses. Last year for DeVille.

1985: Fleetwood Brougham coupe and sedan the sole surviving rear drive models (coupe dropped at mid-model year). Standard vinyl padded roof.

1986: Bright moldings running from leading edges of front fenders back below the beltline to the rear quarters; full-length bright rocker moldings; electro-luminescent opera lamps.

1989: Restyled grille

1990: New, slimmer front bumper rub strips, composite front headlamps; much wider lower body trim strip.

1991: Same body but firmer springs and new deflected-disc shocks for a more controlled ride.

1992: Clear-coat paint finish. Higher spring rates and firmer damping for optional towing package.

1993. Major facelift: new, bolder, egg-crate grille and "power dome" hood; more rounded front bumper with new, stubby bumper guards.

PERFORMANCE AND UTILITY

Average fuel economy was improved by about 2 mpg in 1982 and by another 2 mpg at the end of the 1980s. The 1993 Fleetwood was rated 16/25, which is pretty impressive for a 19-foot-long vehicle, though people paying $37,000 (the '93 price) probably don't worry about how much gas they use. While

useful changes tightened the suspension in 1991, the Brougham and its predecessors always remained Cadillacs of the old school, replete with bountiful interior space and garish furnishings. *Road & Track* called it "just the entity for the many die-hards who buy old-style rear-drive Cadillacs by the pound."

PROBLEM AREAS

These Cadillacs remained what they had always been: roomy, quiet, comfortable and luxurious land yachts, with tolerably good road manners and a silky ride. Workmanship slipped after 1980, improved again in the late 1980s. They were all very resistant to corrosion, thanks to many anti-rust features: more sacrificial zinc in the primer, hot melt sealers to keep water out, bi-metal moldings where stainless steel was laminated to aluminum. Still, Cadillac was never subject to

By 1985 the Fleetwood Brougham was the only rear-wheel-drive Cadillac left in the line, a dramatic change over the past few years. Every year was rumored to be its last, but persistent demand kept it in production.

High, wide and handsome to some eyes, the Brougham soldiered on in 1988, with wire wheels adding to its allure. Styling remained crisp and formal. Bright moldings ran from front fenders back along the flanks; rocket panel moldings were wide and full-length; opera lamps between doors were electro-luminescent.

as many corrosion complaints as other cars. Also, these Caddys are happy to live on unleaded, lower octane modern fuels, which one cannot always say of their predecessors. The 6-liter V-8, which was replaced in 1982 by 4.1, was a troublesome and controversial engine because of its V-8-6-4 arrangement. This was a "modulated displacement" engine featuring an electromechanical system controlled by a microprocessor, which shut down two or four cylinders in response to driving demands. It featured digital electronic fuel injection and self-diagnosis of engine malfunctions. Its lack of reliability was notorious and, though the microprocessor can be disconnected allowing operation as a V-8 only, it was an unnecessary complication. The earlier 7-liter and later 4.1-liter are far preferable. Some road testers said the big Caddys were no less underpowered with the Buick V-6 (1980-82 only). But a V-6 Cadillac in those days seemed a contradiction in terms.

SUMMARY AND PROSPECTS

Specialty packages are important in this series of Cadillac. Look for the Phaeton DeVille (coupe or sedan with convertible-like roof covering and special interior trim), and Coachbuilder Packages (so labeled) in more recent models. The Brougham D'Elegance had pillow style upholstery and interior assist handles. The latter was permanently popular and always opulent. In 1986, for example, the D'Elegance included Dual Comfort seats upholstered in tufted multi-button cloth or optional leather, a leather-trimmed steering wheel, power trunk release, rear reading lights, controlled-cycle wipers, Tampico carpeting, deluxe floor mats, three overhead assist handles and turbine-vaned wheel covers. If gasoline prices take a big upward swing in the mid-1990s, that will probably affect the value of these cars more than the collector market. None of them look like prime investments, but if you like your Caddy's big and comfortable, a low-mileage Brougham will provide satisfaction you can't get this side of a Lincoln Town Car.

The Brougham d'Elegance for 1990, definitely a dinosaur in the eyes of the road-testers, was still selling in vast quantity, though production was tailing off somewhat. Composite headlamps and new bumper/lower body moldings kept the Brougham looking up to date. Moon roof can be seen here.

Through 1984, the Fleetwood limousines (now shorn of their long-running "Seventy-five" designation) looked like this '77 model, which was considerably smaller than the previous long-wheelbase generation. In addition to the sedan version shown, a formal sedan with closed rear roof quarters were offered.

PRODUCTION

	1977	1978	1979	1980	1981	1982
Sedan DeVille	95,421	88,951	93,211	49,188	86,991	86,020
Brougham	28,000	36,800	42,200	29,659		
Coupe DeVille	138,750	117,750	121,890	55,490	62,724	50,130
Fleetwood						
Brougham coupe			2,300			
Limo	1,582	848	2,025	1,612	1,200	1,450
Limo, formal	1,032	682	2,025			
Chassis	1,299	852	864	750	n/a	n/a

	1983	1984	1985	1986	1987	1988
Sedans, 4dr	109,004	107,920	51,701*	49,137*	65,504*	53,130*
Coupes	65,670	50,840	8,336*			
Limo	1,000	1,839				

	1989	1990	1991	1992
Brougham	40,260	33,741	22,289	n/a

* Broughams only 1985-86

157

SPECIFICATIONS

ENGINE (V-8 gasoline)
Type: .... 8-cylinder V-type
Bore x stroke: .... 1977-80: 4.08 x 4.06 in.;
  1981: 3.80 x 4.06 in.; 1982-86: 3.46 x 3.30 in.; 1987-90:
  3.80 x 3.39; 1991: 3.74 x 3.48 in.; 1992-93: 4.06 x 3.39
  (optional 1990-91)
Displacement: ....1977-80: 425 ci; 1981: 368 ci;
  1982-86: 249 ci; 1987-90: 307 ci; 1991: 305 ci; 1992-93:
  350 (optional 1990-91)
Valve operation: ....overhead
Compression ratio: 1977-81: 8.2:1; 1982-86:
  8.5:1; 1987-91: 8:1; 1992-93: 9.3:1
Induction system: .... 1977-80: 2bbl carburetor; fuel
  injection optional; 1981: 4bbl carburetor; ...1981-86: fuel
  injection; 1987-90: 4bbl carburetor; 1991-93: fuel injection
Bhp: .... 1977-79: 180 at 3800 rpm (net), 195 with fuel
  injection; 1980: 150 at 3800 rpm; 1981: 140 at 3800 rpm;
  1982: 125 at 4200 rpm; 1983-86: 135 at 4400 rpm; 1987-
  90: 140 at 3200 rpm; 1991: 170 at 4200 rpm (175 in
  optional 5.7 V-8); 1992-93: 185 at 4200 rpm

CHASSIS AND DRIVETRAIN
Transmission: .... 1977-81: 3spd Turbo Hydra-matic;
  1982-93: 4spd automatic overdrive
Final drive ratio: .... 1977-80: 2.28:1, 3.08:1 optional, std.
  on limo.; 1981: 2.41:1; 1982-85: 3.42:1; 1986: 2.41:1;
  1987: 2.73:1; 1988-90: 2.93:1; 1991-93: 3.08:1
Front suspension: ...... independent, coil springs, tube shocks
Rear suspension: .... live axle, coil springs, tube shocks
Frame: .... full perimeter

GENERAL
Wheelbase: ....121.5 in., limo 144.5 in.
Overall length:................................ 221-225 in., limo 244 in.
Overall width: .... 76-77 in.
Track: .... 62 in. front, 61 in. rear
Tire size: ....1977-83: GR78 x 15, limo HR78 x
  15; 1984-87: P215/75R15; 1988-93: P225/75R15 self-
  sealing
Weight: .... 4000-4400 lbs., limo 4700-4800 lbs.

PERFORMANCE
Acceleration: .... 0-60: 14-16 seconds
Top speed: .... 105 mph
Fuel mileage: .... 1977-81: 14-18 mpg,
  1982-90: 16-22 mpg; 1991: 93: 16-25 mpg

Reskinned in the modern idiom for 1993, the rear-drive Cadillac readopted an old name as the Fleetwood Brougham. This was a dramatic restyle, and an expensive one, suggesting that the Division plans to keep it around for awhile longer. The biggest Cadillac around, it still offers the cavernous interior which earned it popularity.

Chapter 37

Eldorado 1979-85

Eldorado 1979-85
★★ Coupe
★★★ Convertible

HISTORY

The first of three impressive generations of new, lighter Eldorados appeared as a close coupled hardtop coupe for 1979, riding a 114-inch wheelbase, nearly 1,200 pounds lighter, eight inches narrower and twenty inches shorter than its predecessor. Two engines were available: a 350 cid Olds-built V-8 with electronic fuel injection (same as Seville) and a Diesel version of this engine, also by Oldsmobile. Standard Eldorado equipment included such impressive, internationally accepted features as independent rear suspension, disc brakes on all four wheels and electronic level control.

An upgrade package was the Biarritz,

The 1985 El Dorado convertible, second year for this new bodystyle, with power top, glass rear window and rear side windows that raised or lowered automatically with the top. Reinforced frame rails and crossmembers made this a tight ragtop. An electric rear window defogger was optional this year along with spoke aluminum alloy wheels.

which featured a stainless steel half-roof and padded vinyl rear-roof section, plus bright-metal molding along the tops of the front fenders and the line through the rear roof quarters. Wheels were cast aluminum, and opera lamps were standard. The basic, cloth-upholstery Biarritz cost $2,350 extra; leather seats commanded another $350.

For its second year the Eldorado received a new, lighter engine, the 368 (see comments in Chapter 36), producing 145 horsepower and operating with reduced friction and featuring Digital Electronic Fuel Injection (DEFI) on all but California models (which continued with the 350). DEFI consisted of an on-board digital microprocessor and several engine-mounted sensors that monitored various operating functions, metering fuel accordingly, controlling spark timing and diagnosing any engine problems. Two new 1982 variations were the full cabriolet roof, which simulated a convertible top; and the Eldorado Touring Coupe, which featured the sports/touring suspension introduced as a 1981 option, plus special trim (silver paint, black windshield/reveal moldings, silver headlamp and taillamp bezels, gray rubber rocket moldings, black steel-belted radials, aluminum wheels with exposed lugs, leather-wrapped steering wheel, gray leather upholstery, hood badge instead of stand-up ornament). In 1983 the Touring Coupe was available in light brown with a saddle interior. A new 4.1 liter V-8 replaced both the V-8-6-4 and the Buick V-6 that had been optional in 1982.

In 1984 Eldorado offered the first convertible since 1976, the Biarritz, with power top, glass rear window and rear side windows that raised or lowered automatically with the top. Available in white, blue or metallic read, all came with a white top. Frame rails and crossmembers were reinforced, and the body strengthened for rigidity. The top had a color-coordinated cloth headliner and extra sound insulation. An electric defogger for the convertible's glass rear window became optional in 1985, along with a very handsome spoke aluminum alloy wheel for either body style.

IDENTIFICATION

1979: Much shorter and lighter looking than previous Eldos. Large, square grille in egg-crate pattern, squared headlamp. Chrome fender outlines on Biarritz. Cabriolet-style roof with or without padded vinyl.

1980: More complicated grillework with prominent vertical bars.

1981: Finer grillework; large red medallions in wheel covers. New "variable displacement" 368 fuel injected V-8-6-4 (see comments in previous chapter). On-board Computer Diagnostic system.

1982: Three horizontal grille bars; white-center black rub strips on bumper. Cadillac crest on taillights.

1983: Premium sound system. Aluminum wheel option for base Eldorado.

1984: Convertible body style. Bodyside moldings now keyed to exterior color. Catalytic convertor.

1985: No discernable physical changes; consult vehicle identification numbers.

PERFORMANCE AND UTILITY

These Eldorados had outstanding handling and roadability, thanks to front-wheel-drive and a well-designed independent rear suspension (semitrailing arms, coil springs, electronic level control, telescopic shocks and anti-roll bars). The Touring Coupe was yet better with no appreciable loss in ride comfort. The most successful engine was the later 4.1 liter, which had none of the reliability problems that plagued the V-8-6-4 and none of the Diesel sluggishness of Eldorado's optional engine. Though it's not a lot of engine for this much car, what it lacks in performance is compensated by smoothness and precision. Though complex, the 4.1's fuel injection system had a good record for reliability.

PROBLEM AREAS

The biggest problem Cadillac had was with the V-8-6-4 engine, which had a dreadful service record and is definitely not recommended, unless you disconnect the microprocessor and run it as a straight V-8. The overall quality of fit, finish and workmanship was good, though not great. The Diesel was not known for longevity—a contradiction in terms, but there it is. Eldorados seem reasonably rust resistant.

SUMMARY AND PROSPECTS

At the end of 1992, used car market guides were still citing the 1985 Eldo convertible at $10,000 (the 1985 coupe about $5,000), which means that it is holding up fairly well in the trade—after all, they only made 5,600 copies. The convertible will certainly bottom out at about $5,000 for top-condition examples, then start climbing back up. How it will do as a collector car is a longer-term question. It falls into a curious void: an early example of downsizing, but not really high-tech. Collector interest in "modern" convertibles hasn't blossomed the way so many experts were predicting back in the 1980s. People seem to want earlier models for their collectible ragtops. The Touring Coupe is a special car with many good qualities. It should have at least some following ten or twenty years from now. The Biarritz trim option is more akin to traditional Cadillac values, and should also do well.

PRODUCTION

	1979	1980	1981	1982	1983	1984	1985
coupe	67,436	52,685	60,643	52,018	67,416	74,506	74,101
convertible						3,300	2,300

SPECIFICATIONS

ENGINE (V-8 gasoline; Diesel optional)
Type: .... 8-cylinder V-type, cast iron block
Bore x stroke: .... 1979: 4.06 x 3.38 in.;
   1980-81: 3.80 x 4.06 in.; 1982-85: 3.46 x 3.30
Displacement: ....1979: 350 ci;
   1980-81: 368 ci; 1982-85: 250 ci
Valve operation: ....overhead
Compression ratio: 1979: 8:1; 1980-81:
   8.2:1; 1982-85: 8.5:1
Induction system: .... fuel injection
Bhp: .... 1979: 180 at 4200 rpm;
   1980: 145 at 3600 rpm; 1981: 140 at 3600 rpm; 1982:
   190 at 4200 rpm; 1983-85: 135 at 4400 rpm
CHASSIS AND DRIVETRAIN
Transmission: .... 1979-81: 3spd Turbo Hydra-matic;
   1982-85: 4spd automatic overdrive
Final drive ratio: 1979-80: 2.19:1; 1981-82: 2.41:1;
   1983-85: 3.15:1
Front suspension: .... independent, coil springs
Rear suspension: .... independent, trailing arm
Frame: .... full perimeter
GENERAL
Wheelbase: .... 113.9 in.
Overall length:.. 204.0 in.
Overall width: .... 71.4 in.
Track: .... 60.5 in. front and rear
Tire size: P205/75R15
Weight: .... 3,800 lbs.; convertible 3900 lbs.
PERFORMANCE
Acceleration: .... 0-60: 12 seconds
Top speed: .... 110-115 mph
Fuel mileage: .... 17-20 mpg

Chapter 38

Seville 1980-1985

HISTORY

The first redesign of Cadillac's highly successful "international-size" sedan, this was a dramatic piece of work by stylist Wayne Cady. Cady reached into the past—Hooper and Vanden Plas coachwork were the inspiration—for the exotic bustle-back rear deck. He gave the Seville a presence and individuality it had thus far lacked, and seemingly assured its future collectibility. Also new was a vertical-style grille, which blended nicely with the rear end concept. Added to that was a mechanical package that included front-wheel drive and a good V-8 engine (or a not-so-good diesel). Cadillac had outfitted a $21,000 grand luxe carriage that

Bill Mitchell's legacy, the new 1980 Seville, was a daring approach to a modern luxury car—controversial but ultimately accepted. This is the handsomely two-toned Elegante version.

out-dragged and out-rode a Mercedes 300D—and came closer to Mercedes roadability than a casual observer might suspect.

There was a lot of controversy about the Seville in the beginning, but it's become part of the landscape now. Quoting Richard Egan of Goldsmith Cadillac in New York, "It looks more like a Cadillac than it ever did. I think it's the best car we've had in several years. People here aren't scared by the price tag. We're seeing more Mercedes and other foreign buyers." Time, and the overwhelming acceptance of all Cadillacs, is on the side of the new Seville, and it will probably go down as a great collector car of the eighties.

IDENTIFICATION

1980: The first Hooper-style deck. Square, traditional grille. Elegante version continued, with two-tone paint divided by broad bright-molding sweeping from the front to the rear in a plunging French curve, special identification and leather upholstery.

1981: Vertical textured grille. Cast-aluminum wheels standard, chrome wires optional.

1982: No significant exterior changes.

Options included $995 "full cabriolet roof" in black, white or dark blue.

1983: Vertical emphasis on grille toned down. Cadillac script on grille. Clear lenses for parking/turn-signal lamps. New optional aluminum wheels. New optional premium sound system with electronically tuned receiver. Four enclosures for speakers and amplifiers. Dolby noise reduction for tapes.

1984: Horizontal taillights had a clear outer lens and red inner lens. Fine vertical accented grille with Cadillac nameplate in lower left corner. Body colored side moldings.

1985: No exterior changes. Elegante version had two-section "Inner Shield" windshield with plastic layer preventing splinters in accident. Commemorative Edition announced mid-model year—a Seville to look for.

PERFORMANCE AND UTILITY

As for the Eldorado of 1979 to the present, the new Seville was a fine road car, leisurely in acceleration but absolutely quiet at high speed. It was a really great package overall,

Seville Elegante 1981 model. Side view shows novel rear end, most important styling element likely to make post-1979 Sevilles worth saving.

Little change "for the sake of change" occurred at Cadillac in the eighties; the 1983 Seville Elegante was a near match to the 1982.

1980 Seville

ENGINE (1980 DIESEL)

Type: . . . . . 8-cylinder 90° V-type diesel standard, two gas engines optional
Bore x stroke: . . . . 4.06x3.39 in.
Displacement: . . . . 350.0 ci
Valve operation: . . . . overhead
Compression ratio: 22.5:1
Induction system: . . . . electronic fuel injection
Bhp: . . . . 105 at 3200 rpm (net)

CHASSIS AND DRIVETRAIN

Transmission: . . . . Turbo Hydra-matic
Final drive ratio: 2.41:1
Rear suspension: . . . independent, A-arms, coil springs, tube shocks
Front suspension: . . independent, A-arms, coil springs, tube shocks
Frame: . . . . unit body and chassis assembly with sub-frames

GENERAL

Wheelbase: . . . . 113.9 in.
Overall length: . . . . 204.8 in.
Track: . . . . 62.0 in. front and rear
Tire size: P205/75R15
Weight: . . . . 3911 lb.

PERFORMANCE (DIESEL)

Acceleration: . . . . 0-60: 19.0 seconds
Top speed: . . . . 100 mph
Fuel mileage: . . . . 21-23 mpg

and so far ahead of the rival Continental as to be in another class. You have to drive one of these cars—and a Mercedes—to understand just how far Cadillac has come during the past decade.

PROBLEM AREAS

Chiefly, reliability problems are found in the diesel and the V-8-6-4 engines (now discontinued). Other problems exist in the same areas as for the 1979- Eldorado.

SUMMARY AND PROSPECTS

If it were the year 2004, I'd have no trouble awarding these Cadillacs, the Elegante versions in particular, four-star ratings. But it's just too soon to make statements like that. Right now they're holding up well in the used-car market, and showing every sign of appreciating before the decade is out.

Those buying Sevilles with an eye toward collectibility should look for the Elegante

Full cabriolet roof option on a 1984 Cadillac Seville added nothing to the lines but was just novel enough to attract admirers 10 or 20 years down the road.

models and get the best original example they can find, regardless of price; a restoration would be unthinkable in a car this complex and expensive. By all means avoid diesels and V-8-6-4s, and stick to the conventional fuel-injected V-8s, among which both the 350 and the new-in-1983 aluminum V-8 with 4.1 liters (249 cid) are excellent. These cars are strongly recommended, but don't expect them to start appreciating right away. Among 1985s, look for the Commemorative Edition as well as the Elegante.

PRODUCTION	*1980*	*1981*	*1982*	*1983*	*1984*	*1985*
Four-door sedan	39,344	28,631	19,998	30,430	39,997	39,755

New wire wheel design available on 1985 Sevilles. This is probably the worst angle the car has, and it still looks good.

Chapter 39

Cimarron 1982-1988

★ **Cimarron 1982-1988**

HISTORY

The quintessential bad idea, Cimarron was born of unsound reasoning and allowed to happen because auto companies don't employ house historians. If they did, Cadil-

If you think a Cimarron will ever be collectible you are the very soul of optimism; but if it comes to pass, the best bets would be limited editions, like the 1984 D'Oro. Sales have been trailing off, and the Cimarron is probably destined to be phased-out in 1986.

lac would have been reminded that products that go against the grain of tradition are almost always failures. The Cimarron wasn't a bad car, especially after it received a V-6 in 1985. But it was a bad Cadillac. Unlike the front-wheel-drive Eldorado and Seville of the early 1980s, it represented an utter reversal in Cadillac's customer orientation. Though daring, neither the Eldo nor Seville were out of tune with the needs of traditional Cadillac buyers. The Cimarron was.

A gussied-up version of the low-end General Motors J-car, Cimarron had front-wheel-drive, MacPherson-strut front suspension, independent rear with trailing arms and coil springs, unit-body-chassis construction. It was thought to compete with rivals Cadillac had never before considered but was beginning to worry about: the Saab 900, Volvo GL, Audi 5000 and BMW 3-series. But people who bought those cars wouldn't look twice at a GM J-body, while the traditional Cadillac market was turned off by one with a Caddy badge. As for new prospects, J-car admirers could get a Chevy Cavalier or a Buick Skyhawk for many thousands less. Stylewise, too, it was a non-Cadillac, with a 101.2-inch wheelbase and a weight of 2,600 pounds. Performance-wise its initial 1.8 liter four couldn't dust off an out-of-tune DeVille.

168

Cadillac engineers did their best to improve the product over its seven-year life: a two-liter injected four replaced the anemic carburetor 1.8 in 1983; a V-6 became optional in 1985, standard in 1987. The 1987-88 Cimarrons were the best of the lot. But try as it might, Cadillac could not shake the curse of Cimarron's plebian origins. It's not that Cadillac should never have tried a small car; but that if they were going to do it, they should built a ground-up Cadillac, not a Chevy-clone. The problem of the Cimarron was reflected throughout GM in the late 1980s, when the traditional market niches of the five divisions were blurred by overlapping clones.

IDENTIFICATION
1982: Mesh-type egg-crate, horizontal grille with Cadillac badge in center. Small slots in wheels.

1983: Finer mesh grille with larger slots in wheels. Tungsten-halogen driving lights closely flank the front license plate.

1984: New cross-hatched grillework.

1985: Facelifted at front end so as to look less like a Chevy. Longer front end overhang, black inner surfaces for headlamp bezels, optional styled aluminum wheels and electronic instrument cluster.

1986: Facelifted at rear, with new wraparound taillamps.

1987: Flush-mounted composite headlamps, wraparound parking lights on all models. Gray and silver lower body molding.

1988: Fourteen-inch wheels. Body colored lower body molding.

PERFORMANCE AND UTILITY
Cimarrons were quicker beginning 1983, thanks to a larger engine with "swirl" intake ports and cylinder-head, revised camshaft and higher compression, plus an all-new five-speed overdrive manual transmission as standard equipment. But five-speeds are harder to find since (contrary to the marketing game plan) most Cimarrons were ordered with automatics. The V-6 that arrived in 1985 (at first a $610 option, then standard in 1987-88) makes the Cimarron more fun to drive and more like a Cadillac.

Then again, you can buy a V-6 Cavalier in the same model years, and for much less money.

PROBLEM AREAS
J-bodies have not suffered from the reliability problems that plagued the previous X-bodies, and workmanship has always been relatively good. Cadillac spent more time on fit and finish than Chevy and the rest, so the Cimarron was a well-put-together car. Its greatest problems were poor pickup (on the four cylinder jobs), rough idling (especially with the air conditioner on), sloppy shifting, exhaust boom at high rpm, all evidence of lack of refinement.

SUMMARY AND PROSPECTS
In 1992, with the Cimarron four years out of production, a clean 1988 which had sold new for $16,000 was retailing at $6,500, which was quite a drop (a Saab 900 which had sold for the same price was worth $8,500)—yet at that time, you could buy a 1988 Cavalier V-6 coupe for $4,500. These numbers reflect the degree of current interest in used Cimarrons, which does not bode well for their future collectibility. Remember too that they came only as four-door sedans, traditionally the least interesting body style to collectors. Still, J-cars are pleasant enough to drive, reasonably well hung together, and serviceable by any downtown grease monkey. If the Cimarron package appeals to you, and you can find a very nice one, think of it as good transportation.

By 1988 Cimarron was looking more European and aggressive with air dam, flush headlamps, driving lights, body side molding and 14-inch alloy wheels; a V-6 had been offered beginning 1985 and was made standard in 1987. This was Cimarron's last year.

The D'Oro package is worth looking for. This consisted of gold accent stripes and rub strips, gold-accented grille and wheels, foglamp covers, saddle leather seats, gold tinted hood ornament, steering wheel spokes and horn pad emblem. D'Oros were painted red or white, with special plaques.

In 1986 D'Oros received flush mounted composite headlamps and wrap-around parking lights, and in 1987 the D'Oro goodies became standard equipment. The 1988 is the most desirable model year, being the last and the lowest production.

SPECIFICATIONS

ENGINE

Type: 1982-86: 4-cylinder in line, cast iron block; 1985-88: V-6
Bore x stroke: 1982: 3.50 x 2.90 in.; 1983-86: 3.50 x 3.15 in.; 1985-88: 3.50 x 2.99 in.
Displacement: 1982: 112 ci; 1983-86: 121 ci; 1985-88 V-6: 173 ci
Valve operation: ....overhead
Compression ratio: 1982: 9:1; 1983-86: 9.3:1; 1985-88 V-6: 8.9:1
Induction system: .... 1982: 2bbl. carburetor; 1983-88: fuel injection
Bhp: .... 1982: 85 at 5100 rpm; 1983-88: 88 at 4000 rpm; 1985-88 V-6: 125 at 4500 rpm

CHASSIS AND DRIVETRAIN

Transmission: .... 1982: 4spd manual 1983-88: 5spd manual; 1982-88: 3spd automatic optional
Final drive ratio: .... 1982: 3.65:1; 1983-88: 3.83:1; 1982-88 automatic: 3.18:1

Front suspension: .... independent, beam axle, MacPherson struts, coil springs, antiroll bar
Rear suspension: .... independent, trailing arms, coil springs, antiroll bar
Frame: .... unit body and chassis assembly with sub-frames

GENERAL

Wheelbase: ....101.2 in.
Overall length:.. 173.0 in.
Overall width: .... 66.5 in.
Track:.. 55 in. front and rear
Tire size: .... 1982-87: P195/70R13; 1988: P195/70R14; P215/60R14 optional
Weight: .... 2600-2700 lbs.

PERFORMANCE

Acceleration: .... 0-60: 1982: 16 seconds; 1983-86: 15 seconds; 1985-88 V-6 12 seconds
Top speed: .... Four cylinder: 95 mph; V-6: 105 mph
Fuel mileage: .... Four cylinder: 22-26 mpg; V-6: 20-24 mpg

---

PRODUCTION

1982	1983	1984	1985	1986	1987	1988
25,968	19,294	21,898	19,890	24,534	14,561	6,454

Chapter 40

DeVille, 1985-93
Fleetwood, 1985-92
Sixty Special, 1987-93

★ **DeVille, 1985-93**
★ **Fleetwood, 1985-92**
★ **Sixty Special, 1987-93**

HISTORY

Introduced early, the 1985 DeVille/Fleetwood was another product of GM's Roger Smith era, when it was thought appropriate (and there were plenty who thought so besides Mr. Smith) to save money by distributing five or six basic platforms among all the divisions. This offered certain economies of scale, but at a price—diminishment of the individual marque identities from Pontiac to Cadillac that had so well sustained GM for generations. (Chevy's image had blurred earlier, but Chevy was so big that no one noticed.) Thus arrived the all-new front-drive DeVille and Fleetwood, C-body clones to the Buick Electra and Oldsmobile Ninety-Eight, sharing a 110.8-inch wheelbase—unheard of in previous Caddys bearing those names. The Cadillacs' only novel feature was their transverse engines. Included in the lineup was a new Fleetwood Coupe, with standard cabriolet roof, opera lamps

Dramatically shrunken, the 1985 Sedan de Ville didn't go down at all well with traditional customers, and Cadillac quickly began rethinking their design direction. As cars they were very good, excellent performers and much better put together than their recent predecessors.

171

and wire wheel covers. Standard features on all 1985s included "retained power accessory system," which conveniently allowed the power windows and trunk release to work for ten minutes after the ignition was switched off. Anti-lock braking was a new option in 1986, along with a DeVille touring package with handling improvements and sporty trim: gray rocker moldings, front air dam, rear spoiler, foglamps.

A famous name returned after a five-year absence in 1987: the Sixty Special, with its traditional longer wheelbase, stretched five inches from the Fleetwood d'Elegance. Production was only about 2,000. Standard equipment included carpeted rear footrests, twin roof-mounted rear vanity mirrors, and anti-lock braking. The distinction of a longer wheelbase lasted only two years: in 1989,

The Coupe de Ville version of the new front-drive '85, which looked considerably better in two-door format, and is recommended as more collectible.

Another departure from tradition in 1985 was the use of the Fleetwood name on a standard size Cadillac, a slightly better trimmed Sedan de Ville, itself a clone of certain Buicks and Oldsmobiles. Very well fitted out, a low-mileage Fleetwood won't cost much on today's market.

Cadillac shuffled the mix, placing all the four-door models on a 113.8-inch wheelbase while leaving the two-doors on the 110.8. Priced at $31,300, nearly $5,000 more than the Fleetwood, the Sixty Special could only boast a leather interior; heated front seats with power lumbar, thigh and lateral supports; automatic day/night mirror, rear passenger footrests, rear overhead console and vinyl top.

To the extra bulk achieved in 1989, Cadillac added 25 more horsepower in 1990, thanks to multi-point fuel injection and other changes to the 4.5 liter V-8. A Driver's side airbag and GM Pass Key theft-deterrent system were standard; the five model lineup (DeVille and Fleetwood sedan and coupe, Sixty Special sedan) was retained. A significant facelift in 1991 gave the cars a bolder "face" with a prominent egg-crate grille and "power dome" hood, but the severe notchback roofline which many customers didn't like was retained. Aside from a yet-larger 4.9-liter V-8, only minor changes were made in 1992. A traction-control system was a useful addition, and the Touring Sedan package with minimal chrome and firmer ride was an appealing departure. The Fleetwood name was passed over to the rear-drive model in 1993 and the two front-wheel-drive lines were now called simply DeVille and Sixty Special. Cadillac has made commendable improvements in its front-wheel-drive breadwinners over the years, and entering 1993, they were the best selling luxury cars in the United States.

Cadillac reacted to complaints about truncated 1985-86 Fleetwoods by bumping the Sixty Special wheelbase to 115.8 inches in 1987, and applying the five inches extra length to the passenger compartment, a good move on many counts. Euro-style headlamps and longer rear fender caps completed the transformation.

IDENTIFICATION

1985: Very square and truncated compared with previous DeVilles and Fleetwoods. Short, vertical bar grille. Opera lamps and limousine-style back window on Fleetwood.

1986: Grille composed of many thin vertical bars, three larger horizontal bars, with Cadillac script in lower right corner. Touring packages carry "Touring Coupe" or "Touring Sedan" script.

1987: Slightly reshaped grille flanked by Euro-style composite headlamps with combined high/low beams; new rear bumpers and longer fender caps. Fleetwood line consisted of two four-doors: the d'Elegance a new Sixty Special on extended 115.8-inch wheelbase.

1988: Standard 4.5-liter V-8.

1989: Front fenders made of a "nylon composite" material rather than steel. Standard rear shoulder belts. All four-doors now have a 113.8-inch wheelbase, two-doors retain 110.8. Fleetwood coupe returns.

1990: Driver's side airbag and multi-point fuel injection adopted, telescoping steering wheel dropped.

1991: New 4.9-liter engine. Bolder, eggcrate-style grille with prominent vertical bars. "Power dome" hood. Fifteen-inch cast aluminum wheels. Identify later models by VIN numbers.

1992: Black body-side rub moldings. Traction control.

The 1989 Sedan de Ville looked elegant in black, and was more spacious, on its three-inch-longer wheelbase. Sales had picked up considerably by now, so these Cadillacs are relatively plentiful on today's used car market—go for one with very low mileage.

Handsome and sleek, the 1989 Fleetwood Sixty Special displays its formal lines. All four-doors were now on the 113.8-inch wheelbase, which meant the 60S actually took a decrease in size, but it's not apparent on the inside thanks to clever seat design and placement.

The Coupe de Ville version of the 1989 restyle retained the original 110.8-inch wheelbase but got away with it thanks to its wide doors. Interestingly, though, the sedans were outselling the coupes now, an inversion of the usual Cadillac body style proportion.

The 1991 Fleetwood, displaying that year's major facelift, giving Cadillac a bolder frontal apparance and emphasizing its "power dome" hood. Notchback roofline continued to look odd, however, and was not popular.

1993: Redesigned, more aerodynamic wheel covers with less prominent blades.

PERFORMANCE AND UTILITY

Putting the 4.1 liter V-8 in a car two feet shorter and 600 pounds lighter did wonders for performance. While the jumbo Brougham did 0-60 in 15 seconds, the new Fleetwood did it in 12 seconds, and average fuel mileage was up about three miles per gallon. These Cadillacs offer more responsive handling and a well-controlled ride that isn't as soft or floaty as the Brougham, but they do not challenge European sports sedans in handling since there is little roll stiffness and too much understeer. Also, unlike the Brougham, they don't hold six people, or much luggage.

PROBLEM AREAS

Quality control was stressed throughout the life of the front-wheel-drive Cadillacs, and few recalls or catastrophic ailments have been noted.

SUMMARY AND PROSPECTS

As collector cars, it is much too early to judge these Cadillacs. Who knows? They may one day speak to old-car-folk the way a 1953 Sixty Special speaks today. Still, they remain basically sedans, and workaday body styles have never set collector juices running. Consider them strictly used cars for the foreseeable future.

The 1993 Sedan de Ville, had a cleaner grille. Beginning 1992, de Villes used the larger 4.9-liter V-8; a traction-control system was usefully adopted.

PRODUCTION

	1985	1986	1987	1988	1989	1990	1991
four-doors	114,278	129,857					
two-doors	37,485	36,350					
total			162,798	152,513	178,938	176,589	147,998

SPECIFICATIONS

ENGINE (V-8 gasoline; Diesel optional 1985 only)
Type: .... 8-cylinder V-type, aluminum block
Bore x stroke:............. 1985-87: 3.46 x 3.30 in.; 1988-90: 3.62 x 3.31 in.; 1991-93: 3.62 x 3.62 in.
Displacement: ....1985-87: 249 ci; 1988-90: 273 ci; 1991-93: 300 ci
Valve operation: ....overhead
Compression ratio: 1985-90: 9:1; 1991-93: 9.5:1
Induction system: .... 1985-89: throttle body fuel injection; 1990-93: multi-point fuel injection
Bhp: .... 1985: 125 at 4200 rpm; 1986-87: 130 at 4200 rpm; 1988-89: 155 at 4000 rpm; 1990: 180 at 4300 rpm; 1991-93: 200 at 4100 rpm

CHASSIS AND DRIVETRAIN
Transmission: .... 4spd automatic overdrive
Final drive ratio: 1985-89: 2.97:1, 1990-93: 2.73:1

Front suspension: .... independent, MacPherson struts, lower control arms, coil springs, stabilizer bar
Rear suspension: .... independent, struts, coil springs, stabilizer bar, electronic level control
Frame: .... unit body/chassis with subframes

GENERAL
Wheelbase: ....1985-88: 110.8 in.; 1987-88 60S: 115.8 in.; 1989-93 4drs: 113.8 in. ; 1989-93 2drs: 110.8 in.
Overall length:............. 1985-88: 195.0 in.; 1987-88 60S: 201.5; 1989-93 4drs: 205 in.; 1989-93 2drs: 205 in.
Overall width: .... 71-72 in.
Track: .... 60.3 in. front, 59.8 in. rear
Tire size: P205/75R14, P205/70R15 (1989)
Weight: .... 3400-3600 lbs.

PERFORMANCE
Acceleration:.. 0-60: 10-12 seconds
Top speed: .... 110 mph
Fuel mileage: .... 16/25 mpg

The Sixty Special made one of its periodic reappearances in 1993, when the Fleetwood name was transferred to the rear-drive model. Rear skirts and conservative wheelcovers differentiated this car from the breadwinner Sedan de Ville—but it did look like the traditional Sixty Special we all knew and loved.

Chapter 41

Fleetwood Seventy-Five, 1985-87

★ **Fleetwood Seventy-Five, 1985-87**

HISTORY

Proof positive that Cadillac's general approach had changed forever was the first downsized, front-wheel-drive limousine in Division history, built on a stretched C-car platform based on the chassis of the new 1985 DeVille and Fleetwood. The body started as a Fleetwood coupe, was stretched nearly two feet to accommodate up to eight people, which was no fewer than the big rear-drive limousine that was discontinued. Compared to the latter, the new Fleetwood was nearly 26 inches shorter and 1,200 pounds lighter. Drivetrain was identical to the DeVille/Fleetwood coupes and sedans. Standard features included rear control panels that allowed passengers to unlatch the rear doors, climate control, and remote con-

A Fleetwood coupe, stretched nearly two feet was the basis of the new 1985 Fleetwood Seventy-five limousine, complete with modern front-wheel-drive and capable of housing eight people, despite being 26 inches shorter and 1,200 pounds lighter than the previous limos.

trols for the stereo and cassette player. A seven-passenger formal sedan with closed rear roof quarters was introduced later in the year. The Diesel engine initially available in the DeVille/Fleetwood was never offered. Since 1987, manufacture of Cadillac limousines has been handled by specialist builders, so these Seventy-Fives represent the end of a long and distinguished line of in-house professional cars, and a model that can be traced back over fifty years.

IDENTIFICATION

1985: Obviously shorter than previous limousines; rear doors have dividers; vinyl half roof with opera windows, closed on formal sedans.

PERFORMANCE AND UTILITY

The new Seventy-Five accommodated as many passengers as before with much less bulk, but still required nearly a 50-foot turning circle, so maneuverability can't be cited as superb. The obvious comparison is to the Chrysler K-car limousines, also front-drive; against those, Cadillac offered the advan-tage of a V-8 engine, wonderful silence at all speeds, and a superb ride.

PROBLEM AREAS

The major problem is the usual one for such low production cars: the lack of spare body and trim parts. However, Cadillac has always been committed to stocking parts for its formal cars a long time, and no limousine is so old that the bits and pieces can't be obtained through the dealer parts network. The service record of these limos has been very good.

SUMMARY AND PROSPECTS

Again, with a car this recent it is too soon to say anything about potential collectibility, though it seems that its diminished bulk would recommend it to future collectors who don't have the room for its enormous predecessors.

PRODUCTION

1985	1986	1987
405	1,000	1,000 est.

The 1987 Fleetwood Seventy-five was virtually unchanged from its initial year, but this was to be its last appearance. Closed roof quarters could also be ordered this year.

SPECIFICATIONS

ENGINE

Type: .... 8-cylinder V-type, aluminum block
Bore x stroke: .... 3.46 x 3.30 in.
Displacement: ....249 ci
Valve operation: ....overhead
Compression ratio: 9:1
Induction system: .... throttle body fuel injection
Bhp: .... 1985: 125 at 4200 rpm; 1986-87: 135 at 4400 rpm

CHASSIS AND DRIVETRAIN

Transmission: .... 4spd automatic overdrive
Final drive ratio: 2.97:1
Front suspension: .... independent, MacPherson struts, lower control arms, coil springs, stabilizer bar

Rear suspension: .... independent, struts, coil springs, stabilizer bar, electronic level control
Frame: .... unit body/chassis with subframes

GENERAL

Wheelbase: .... 134.4 in.
Overall length:.. 218.6 in.
Overall width: .... 71.7 in.
Track: .... 60.3 in. front, 59.8 in. rear
Tire size: P205/75R14, P205/70R15 (1989)
Weight: .... 3400-3600 lbs.

PERFORMANCE

Acceleration: .... 0-60: 12-14 seconds
Top speed: .... 105 mph
Fuel mileage: .... 14/22 mpg

Chapter 42

Eldorado, Seville, 1986-91

★ **Eldorado, Seville, 1986-91**

HISTORY

In 1986, GM bet that it could sell smaller and more expensive versions of the E-body (Eldorado and Seville in Cadillac's case) to the very people it had brought up to buy 'em by the pound. So the humpback Seville and razoredge Eldo were replaced a new body 16 inches shorter and 350 pounds lighter. The Eldorado looked reasonably evolutionary, but the Seville was a complete departure from the radical and distinctive humpback of 1980-85.

GM lost its bet. What appeared appropriate on paper failed to take into account what the customers had been educated to believe. Sales fell by a staggering 60 percent, and GM reportedly lost a million dollars a day with the E-body alone.

Hastily, Cadillac reskinned the two models in 1988. The Eldorado had the more extensive facelift, gaining three inches in length, and nearly doubled its sales as a result. It took the Seville longer to recover. But neither model sold anywhere near the level of its preceding generation, which had done about double their number, even in recession years 1979-81.

The downsized, lighter Eldorado Biarritz for 1986 was totally underwhelming in its sales performance, and Cadillac almost immediately began to plan changes. Aluminum V-8, automatic overdrive and all-wheel independent suspension gave it competent performance and handling, but people could not get excited about the shape and size of the thing.

Built on the Eldorado platform from 1986 was the truncated new Seville (1987 model shown here), which had a severe identity crisis after six years of radical "humpbacks" with styling taken from classic English themes. It ought to be possible to buy a low-mileage Seville like this for little money.

Both cars were built on the same chassis as the new Buick Riviera and Oldsmobile Toronado, but both managed to retain a distinct Cadillac look. They were unique for their standard, transverse-mounted 4.1 liter V-8, two-sided galvanized metal for all exterior body panels except the roof, and flush-mounted composite headlamps with high- and low-beam bulbs in a single assembly. There was four-wheel independent suspension, disc brakes at each corner, a novel transverse single fiberglass rear leaf spring. Standard features included a floor-mounted shift lever, digital instrument cluster with driver information center (tachometer and engine gauges), and a tilt/telescoping steering wheel. Genuine walnut veneer was standard on all Sevilles and the Eldorado Biarritz, and a cellular telephone was among the options. But, to the regret of collectors, there was no convertible.

For 1990 there was a mild facelift, driver's side airbag and more horsepower, thanks to multi-point fuel injection (one injector for each cylinder) instead of throttle-body injection (two injectors mounted atop engine). Compression went up to 9.5:1, requiring premium gas. Minor trim changes and a few new gadgets were applied. A novel idea was the "central unlocking system": this allowed all doors to be unlocked if the key was held in a turned position for 1.5 seconds on either front door. A rear window defogger, heated outside mirrors and illuminated entry system were made standard on all models; anti-lock brakes were standard on the STS,

optional on others. Cadillac improved the breed again in 1991. The standard engine grew to 4.9 liters and 200 horsepower and delivered to the wheels through an excellent new electronically controlled four-speed automatic transmission. Computer Command Ride (CCR), Cadillac's new speed-dependent damping system, was standard—shock firmness increased with vehicle speed. Anti-lock brakes and driver's side airbags were standard on all models, while the STS and Eldo Touring Coupe had standard leather and elm interior trim.

IDENTIFICATION

1986: All new and drastically downsized; Seville drops humpback styling for conventional notchback; clean egg-crate grille, composite headlamps.

1987: Slightly taller, 75-series tires, hydro-elastic (instead of rubber) engine mounts. VIN numbers marked on all major body panels. No obvious visual changes.

1988: New sheet metal; higher, blunter hood with "power dome"; new front fenders with sharp edges on Eldorado; new bumper guards and header molding on Seville. New Seville Touring Sedan.

1989: Maple interior trim on Seville and Eldorado Biarritz, optional on base Eldorado. Graphic equalizer added to sound system. New 155 hp engine.

1990: Cadillac crest and laurel wreath in

Eldorado was considerably reskinned for 1988 with a higher, blunter, "power-dome" hood and crisper fenderlines, an effort to recover some of the Eldo "look" that had pleased buyers before the 1986 restyle. Sales nearly doubled—Cadillac was on the right track.

The good looking Seville Touring Sedan (STS) for 1989. Introduced the year before, the STS. Only about 3,000 of these were built, with one-tone paint job, a tighter suspension, leather seats and burl elm interior trim; seating only four, STS was a stab at the Euro/yuppie-car market. A nice car, and rare: look for it.

center of grille; new bumper moldings. Driver's side airbag.

1991: No external changes. New 4.9-liter, 200 hp V-8; ABS standard.

PERFORMANCE AND UTILITY

Digital instrument cluster contains little information (speed, fuel level, odometer only) and neither model has enough rear-seat and trunk space. STS suspension is very stiff. Quality strongly improved in 1990, along with performance (at the expense of gas mileage). Best performing models are the STS and Touring Coupe for 1991.

PROBLEM AREAS

Neither car suffered much from mechanical problems, but it is too early to make judgments about their long-term longevity.

SUMMARY AND PROSPECTS

Look for the up-market Eldo Biarritz and Seville Elegante trim packages and, after 1988, the sporty Seville Touring Sedan (STS), which saw only about 1,500 copies in '88 and 3,000 a year thereafter. STS features include monochrome exterior, shorter final-drive ratio for quicker acceleration, tauter suspension, high-performance tires on alloy wheels, leather seats, burl elm interior trim and four-passenger seating. When it became known that new designs were planned for 1992, dealers offered big discounts on 1991 models, and they took a terrific dive in value: one year after it sold at a whopping $38,000 sticker, the STS was pegged at $19,000 by the used car value guides; the Eldorado, which sold for $32,000, was around the same level. This depreciation has continued, so it might be possible to pick one up very cheaply now. Potential collectibility is, however, a big question mark.

PRODUCTION

	1986	1987	1988	1989	1990	1991
Eldorado	21,342	17,775	33,210	30,925	22,291	16,212
Seville	19,098	18,578	22,968	22,909	33,128	26,431

By 1990 the Eldorado had recovered much of its former prestige through aggressive, extroverted styling that buried memories of the underwhelming '86. Crest and laurel wreath, seen on the '89 Seville STS, was applied to all Eldos, which also had a driver's side airbag.

SPECIFICATIONS

ENGINE

Type: .... 8-cylinder V-type, aluminum block
Bore x stroke: .... 1986-87: 3.46 x 3.30 in. ;
   1988-90: 3.62 x 3.31 in.; 1991: 3.62 x 3.62
Displacement:..1986-87: 249 ci; 1988-90: 273 ci; 1991: 300 ci
Valve operation: ....overhead
Compression ratio:..1985: 8.5:1; 1986-89: 9:1; 1990-91: 9.5:1
Induction system: .... 1985-89: throttle body fuel injection;
   1990-91: multi-point fuel injection
Bhp: .... 1986-87: 130 at 4200 rpm; 1988-89: 155 at 4000
   rpm; 1990: 180 at 4300 rpm; 1991: 200 at 4100 rpm

CHASSIS AND DRIVETRAIN

Transmission: .... 4spd automatic overdrive
Final drive ratio: 1985-89: 2.97:1; 1990-91:
   2.73:1; 1988-91 STS/TC: 3.31:1
Front suspension: .... independent, MacPherson
   struts, coil springs, stabilizer bar

Rear suspension: .... independent, transverse leaf
   spring, struts, electronic level control
Frame: .... unit body/chassis with subframes

GENERAL

Wheelbase: ....1986: 108 in.
   Overall length:............ 1986-89: 188 in.; 1990-91: 191 in.
Overall width: .... 1986-87: 71 in.; 1988-91: 72 in.
Track: .... 59.9 in. front and rear
Tire size: 1986: P205/75R14; 1987-88:
   P205/75R15 1989-91: P205/70R15; 1988-90 STS/TC:
   P205/70R15; 1991 STS/TC: P215/65R16 Eagle GT+4
Weight: .... 3400-3500 lbs.

PERFORMANCE

Acceleration: .... 0-60: 1986-89: 10-12 seconds;
   1990: 9 seconds; 1991: 8.2 seconds
Top speed: .... 1986-89: 110 mph; 1990-91: 115 mph
Fuel mileage: .... 1986-89: 16/25 mpg 1990-91: 15/23 mpg

New grille with thin vertical bars and crisp rather than rounded lines were a Seville characteristic in 1990 and 1991 (the '91 is shown). Anti-lock brakes were now standard. This was a competent car, but in the period under discussion, the Eldorado has far more collector potential.

Chapter 43

Eldorado, Seville, 1992-93

| ✔ Eldorado, Seville, 1992-93 |
| ★ 1993 Northstar V-8 |

HISTORY

On the same wheelbase as before, Cadillac invested in a major facelift of the E-body platform in 1992, moving in the opposite direction of the past decade: "upsizing," if you will. The 1992s were therefore longer, wider, heavier and even taller, with 11 inches more overhang for the Eldorado. But, while the Seville profile was softened, the Eldorado featured the crisp, angular lines

Seville STS for 1993 displays the rounded, faintly Jaguaresque lines of the current body; introduced in 1992, this was certainly the most effective Seville restyle since the '80 model, but prices have galloped betimes, and it will be years before collectibility of this one can be judged.

that had marked it since its rebirth as a personal-luxury coupe 25 years before—the worst component of which was a clumsy, triangular "C" pillar that prevented good rearward visibility. The usual Eldorado combination of standard luxury model and monochromatic Touring Coupe were offered, while Seville mimicked this approach with its standard sedan and Special Touring edition. The interior was completely redesigned, with the goal of placing all interior controls within the reach of 95 percent of all drivers. The plan succeeded, but at the expense of burying the climate controls in under the steering wheel. The wood trim was genuine cut-from-a-tree wood, which looked a lot better than GM's usual plastic variety. The unit body/chassis was reinforced to provide greater structural rigidity, and thoroughly soundproofed, the Eldorado producing only 67 decibels at 70 mph. Handling was a good combination between stability and comfort, and the Touring Coupe could be thrown into tight corners with complete confidence.

In 1993, with electronically controlled, interactive four-speed automatic; road-sensing, adjustable shock-absorber damping; multilink rear suspension; speed-sensing, variable-boost steering; traction control and four-wheel anti-lock brakes, Cadillac added the piece de resistance, the 4.6-liter Northstar V-8 out of Allante´, bristling with valves and cams, developing nearly 300 net horsepower, and capable of propelling the cars toward the 150 mph mark. This was certainly not your father's Eldorado, or Seville. Of course, they both cost a small fortune, but Cadillac had cleverly placed them quite a few thousand under their Lexus/Infiniti rivals, not to mention those from Germany. These are splendid Cadillacs. The Standard of the World was back.

IDENTIFICATION

No exterior differences. VIN Numbers:

1992 Eldorado: 1G6EL1 () B () N () 000001-up

1992 Seville: 1G6KS5 () B () N () 000001-up; STS: 1G6KY5 () B () N () 000001-up

1993 Eldorado: 1G6EL1 () B () P () 000001-up

1993 Seville: 1G6KS5 () B () P () 000001-up; STS: 1G6KY5 () B () P () 000001-up

PERFORMANCE AND UTILITY

The Seville is the better styling job, a deft compromise between the jellybean school and traditional crisp edges; darker colors suit it best, emphasizing its understated elegance. The Zebrano wood trim and soft leather of the STS are beautiful, and practical. Unfortunately, they've overdone the STS's body-color grille—standard models with their finer mesh, unpainted grilles, will age better. The Eldorado is more Eighties-American-hardtop in its look, with too chunky a back end and square rear side windows that remind you of the clumsy notchback Devilles. Both cars are great drivers, quiet, tight, competent and quick. The Northstar V-8 (optional from 1993) is a revelation, completing a specification that could come from Stuttgart or Munich, but doesn't. Road & Track: "This powerplant gathers itself up in a delicious, heady swoosh to a 6500-rpm crescendo, again and again, wide-open-throttle upshifts best detected by the determined sweep of the analog tachometer. On brief sprints up to 130 mph, both cars felt rock steady."

PROBLEM AREAS

Poor fit between body panels or body and bumpers, and the occasional orange peel, are not serious, except in the Seville's market territory. You don't find these problems on a Lexus.

SUMMARY AND PROSPECTS

The Northstar V-8 is a milestone engine, built in smallish quantities, and I have no doubt that it will make for collectible automobiles twenty years from now. But then is not now. Today, these cars are brand new and very expensive, and hardly worth buying to "put away." It will be years before they recover from their normal depreciation in the 1990s. Still, if you're looking for a new car which represents the state-of-the-art, and a ninety-year tradition, the new Eldorado and Seville deserve your attention.

SPECIFICATIONS

ENGINE

Type: .... 8-cylinder V-type, aluminum block; 1993 option: all aluminum twin-cam V-8
Bore x stroke: ....1992-93: 3.62 x 3.62; 1993 option: 3.66 x 3.31 in.
Displacement: ....300 ci; 1993 option: 279 ci
Valve operation: ....overhead
Compression ratio: ....1992-93: 9:1; 1993 option: 10.3:1
Induction system: .... multi-point fuel injection
Bhp.............. 1992-93: 200 at 4300 rpm; 1993 option: 290 at 5600 rpm

CHASSIS AND DRIVETRAIN

Transmission: .... 4spd automatic overdrive
Final drive ratio: .... 1992-93: 3.33:1; 1993 option: 3.71:1
Front suspension: .... independent, MacPherson struts, lower A-arms, coil springs, adjustable tubular shocks, stabilizer bar

Rear suspension: .... independent, struts, lower A-arms, transverse leaf spring, adjustable tubular shocks, automatic ride leveling
Frame: .... unit body/chassis

GENERAL

Wheelbase: .... 108 in.
Overall length:................... Eldorado: 202 in.; Seville: 204 in.
Overall width: .... 75 in.
Track: .... 60.9 in. front and rear
Tire size: P225/60R16 97H
Weight: .... Eldorado: 3600 lbs.; Seville: 3650 lbs.

PERFORMANCE

Acceleration: .... 0-60: 8.5 seconds; with 1993 Northstar V-8: / seconds
Top speed: .... 120 mph; with 1993 Northstar V-8: 140 mph (factory claims 150)
Fuel mileage:.............. 16/25 mpg; with 1993 Northstar V-8: 15/22 mpg.

Chapter 44

Allanté 1987-93

Allanté 1987-93	
★★	1987-92
★★★	1993

HISTORY

The Cadillac Allanté began as a 1982 concept project called LTS ("Luxury Two-Seater"). In the tradition of the 1953 Eldorado, it developed as a luxury line-leader, but unlike the latter, it was expected to return a profit at about 6,000 units per year, winning conquest sales such rivals as the Mercedes-Benz 560SL, which it distinctly resembled. Built on a shortened Eldorado platform, the handsome, chiseled body was mounted on chassis by Pininfarina in Italy with the drivetrain and final assembly handled in Detroit. Cars flew back and forth between Detroit and Turin via 747 cargo jets.

On introduction in 1987, Allanté became

Spot the differences in this '89 Allanté from the '87? You can't, because the changes were all under the skin—a larger engine was the main one. Cadillac by this time was desperately underpinning the Allanté's used car value, but management was fast becoming disenchanted with the whole project.

186

the first front-wheel-drive car to offer antilock braking as standard—and the first Cadillac with a wheelbase under 100 inches since 1908. Its 4.1-liter V-8 bore only a superficial resemblance to the standard version. Equipped with multi-point fuel injection, roller lifters, high-flow heads and tuned intake manifolds, it developed 170 bhp instead of the standard 130. It also offered rack-and-pinion steering, four-wheel automatic transaxle, and all-strut suspension with front coil springs and anti-roll bar and transverse rear fiberglass leaf springs. Inside were ten-way Recaro leather sets, automatic climate control, a "Driver Information Center" and both digital and analog gauges. An aluminum hardtop with rear window defroster was standard, though the soft-top was manual, which seemed bizarre on a $54,000 car. But the only option was a cellular telephone.

On paper it all seemed very promising, but Cadillac either missed the target, or the target was never there. Many people had never bought anything but European products in this market niche. Cadillac barely sold half its intended number in the first year. Sales were worse in 1988, when the

only changes were a power trunklid pull-down and full-analog gauges as a no-cost option. The base price had then exceeded $56,000, but dealers were happy to sell many of them at under $50,000. Sales continued lackluster in 1989 despite notable improvements, including a larger and more powerful engine, a lower final-drive ratio for better acceleration, speed-sensing power steering and auto-adjusting shocks. Cadillac began to get desperate, offering a "guaranteed resale" price based on the higher resale values of the Mercedes SL. (Trade your Allanté in for another Cadillac, and Cadillac would meet the difference between its value and that of an SL of the same year.) None of this helped, and neither did a lower base price when the hardtop was made optional. Temptations like the first standard traction-control in a front-drive car, a compact disc player and a sophisticated automatic shock damping system failed to create sales inroads. The 1991s debuted with nothing new except a premium sound system and minor mechanical tweaks, but they cost even more and sales were worse than ever. Barely 600 1992s had been built before Cadillac scrubbed them in January of that year, launching the most radical and best Allanté for its last hurrah.

By every measure the 1993 was a great automobile—the kind that comes along once or twice a decade. Its twin cam, 32 valve Northstar V-8 was Cadillac's first all-new

The powerplant that transformed Allanté, 1993's 32-valve Northstar 4.6 liter V-8 with 295 bhp, gave the two-seater a top speed nudging 150 mph. To the consternation of many, Cadillac gave up on the Allanté this year, after finally installing the kind of engine it should have had in the first place.

One piece door glass, new wheels with Z-rated tires, a front air dam and "Northstar 32V" plaques on front fenders easily identify the 1993 Allanté, last of the line. Road-Sensing Suspension varies shock rates, producing a smooth ride without sacrificing handling. This is one great automobile. I wish I could afford it. . . .

engine in ten years, a state-of-the-art unit with 295 *net* horsepower, delivering 0-60 times in the *gran turismo* class and with a top speed close to 150 mph. The automatic transaxle was a strong 4T80E, specially developed for this application; Allanté traction-control was so sophisticated that it could apply the brakes simultaneously with throttling back power. The new Road-Sensing Suspension (RSS) could vary shock rates in 10-15 milliseconds through monitoring sensors. The ride, which had been criticized as harsh in previous models, was now smooth and quiet; yet nothing had been sacrificed in what one tester called the Allanté's "magnificent cornering capabilities...far beyond the confidence of most drivers without a SCCA competition license."

Even dyed-in-the-wool skeptics must wonder why GM does what it does, when it does. In the 1993 Allanté they produced the kind of car people who spend $60,000 expect—"arguably the best front-drive car in the world," as *Road & Track* put it. Then in November 1992, they announced that it was the end of the line. After 3500 copies of this *wundercar* have been built, the Allanté will be gone forever. I can't figure it out.

Sure, GM is in trouble, and looking for ways to shave expenses. But against the kind of stuff they've been palming off under the proud name of Cadillac for the last ten or twenty years, the Allanté is one item in the lineup they should keep, like the 1993 Seville STS and Eldorado Touring Coupe, to inspire and restore our faith in the grand old marque.

This is a splendid automobile, a fit coda to Cadillac's ninety years of automotive history. Its supporters should have fought harder for its survival.

IDENTIFICATION

Rely on VIN numbers in correctly dating Allantes, since physical changes were few:

Cars with hardtop and softtop:
1987: 1G6VR3 () () () H () 000001-up
1988: 1G6VR3 () () () J () 100001-up
1989: 1G6VR3 () 5 () K () 000001-up
1990: 1G6VR3 () 8 () L () 100001-up
1991: 1G6VR3 () 8 () M () 100001-up
1992: 1G6VR3 () 8 () N () 100001-up

Cars with softtop only:
1990: 1G6VS3 () 8 () L () 100001-up
1991: 1G6VS3 () 8 () M () 100001-up
1992: 1G6VS3 () 8 () N () 100001-up
1993: One-piece door glass, new design wheels with Z-rated tires, deeper front air dam, "Northstar 32V" fender plaques.

PERFORMANCE AND UTILITY

Pre-Northstar Allante's are pleasant if firmly-sprung luxury two-seaters with a modicum of performance, very good build quality and distinctive good looks. The 1993 is almost a ready made classic. The softtop received a gas-assisted cover opener and power header latch, but it was still a pain to return it to the well manually. There's a bit of cowl shake, even in the 1993. Understeer, and the tendency to run wide on hard, fast corners, are typical of front-drive but easily corrected.

PROBLEM AREAS

Harsh ride and cowl shake have been the leading customer complaints. It is too early to make longterm judgments about weak points; reader comments are invited. Tire and road noise is commonly noted through 1992, but absent on the 1993 models.

SUMMARY AND PROSPECTS

All Allantés, by their very dearth of numbers, will become collectible. As of late 1992, average used car market price of an original 1987 was around $17,500, while the 1991 had tumbled from its original $60,000 to about $38,000. It would be safe to wait until they hit $10,000 before acquiring a nice example. The 1993 is a Cadillac ranking with such past triumphs as the 1975 and 1980 Seville, the 1967 and 1953 Eldorados, the 1949 V-8s and the tailfinned 1948s. It is "collectible" right now, although, of course, it will be subject to typical depreciation of new cars for six or eight years. After that, I would expect its value to level off and quickly start climbing again. The trick will be to buy at bottom. That should be around $20,000 for an immaculate low-mileage 1993 in, say, 2001. But we speak in 1993 dollars, unadjusted for future inflation...

PRODUCTION

1987	1988	1989	1990	1991	1992	1993
3,363	2,569	3,298	3,101	2,500	624	3,500 est.

SPECIFICATIONS

ENGINE
Type: .... 1987-92: 8-cylinder V-type, aluminum block; 1993: all aluminum twin-cam V-8
Bore x stroke: .... 1987-88: 3.46 x 3.30 in.; 1989-92: 3.62 x 3.31; 1993: 3.66 x 3.31 ln.
Displacement: ....1987-88: 249 ci; 1989-92: 273 ci; 1993: 279 ci
Valve operation: ....overhead
Compression ratio:1987-88: 8.5:1; 1989-92: 9:1; 1993: 10.3:1
Induction system: .... multi-point fuel injection
Bhp: .... 1987-88: 170 at 4300 rpm; 1989 92: 200 at 4300 rpm; 1992: 290 at 5600 rpm

CHASSIS AND DRIVETRAIN
Transmission: .... 4spd automatic overdrive
Final drive ratio: 1987-88: 2.95:1; 1989-92: 3.21:1; 1993: 3.71:1
Front suspension: .... independent, MacPherson struts, lateral and trailing links, coil springs, stabilizer bar

Rear suspension: .... 1987-92: independent, MacPherson struts, H-control arm, transverse leaf spring; 1993: independent, upper and lower control arms, electronic dampers, lateral link.
Frame: .... unit body/chassis

GENERAL
Wheelbase: .... 99.4 in.
Overall length:.. 178.6 in.
Overall width: .... 73.4 in.
Track: .... 60.5 in. front and rear
Tire size: .... 1987-88: P225/60VR15 Eagle VL; 1989-92: P225/55VR16; 1993: P225/60ZR-16 Eagle GA
Weight: .... 1987-92: 3500-3600 lbs.; 1993: 3740 lbs.

PERFORMANCE
Acceleration: .... 0-60: 1987-88: 9.5 seconds; 1989-92: 8 seconds; 1993: 6.5 seconds
Top speed: .... 1987-92: 130 mph; 1993: 145 mph
Fuel mileage: .... 1987-92: 15/22 mpg; 1993: 14/21 mpg

Allanté for 1990, another repeat of the original. Low in production, unique in character, the two-seater Cadillac is destined for collectibility in the long run, but it will take many years to redeem your investment in one of the recent models because of their still-declining value.

Cadillac ownership

Cadillac LaSalle Club Inc.
3340 Poplar Drive
Warren, MI 48091
(313) 755-4621
The oldest and largest Cadillac club was founded
in 1958 and presently numbers 3,000 members.
Membership is open to owners of Cadillacs and
LaSalles through the 1983 model year. The club
publishes a monthly magazine, *The Self-Starter*, a
deluxe *Self-Starter Annual*, and a bi-annual direc-
tory of members. The club maintains model ros-
ters and offers a technical service to cope with
restoration and maintenance problems. Dues are
currently $20 per year in USA, $23 in Canada and
Mexico, and $25 in all other countries.

Brougham Owners Association
829 West Wesley Road
Atlanta, GA 30327
Founded by prominent Brougham collector Cy
Strickler, this is a small but active organization
for owners of Cadillac Eldorado Broughams of all
four model years, 1957 through 1960. Membership is recommended for anyone who owns or
intends to own an Eldorado Brougham. Publica-
tions and technical assistance are offered.

Cadillac Convertible Owners of America
PO Box 920
Thiells, NY 10984
This organization comprises 500 owners or
would-be owners of Cadillac convertibles, and
has been in existence since 1977. Technical and
restoration assistance with special concentration
on convertible problems are offered. Dues are
currently $35 per year.

PARTS & MANUALS
Aabar's Cadillac & Lincoln Salvage
9700 N.E. 23rd
Oklahoma City, OK 73141
(405) 769-3318

Cadillac & LaSalle Service Books
PO Box 17321
West Hartford, CT 06117
Reproduces original shop, service, parts and data
books for all models through 1982.

Cadillac Parts Ltd.
PO Box 6795
Reno, NV 89503
(702) 747-3447
Offers parts, literature and manuals.

HMS Enterprises
PO Box 5251
Takoma Park, MD 20912
(202) 829-0374
Reproduction parts for postwar Cadillacs through
the 1956 model year.

Ted M. Holcombe
2933 Century Lane
Bensalem, PA 19020
(215) 245-4560
Offers both NOS and used parts for 1950-74
model Cadillacs.

John Lindhardt
81-10 190th Street
Jamaica, NY 11423
(718) 740-2877 after 7 pm
Flathead V-8 engine parts.

Robert Mannino
340 East 57th Street
New York, NY 10022
(212) 486-1299
Sells carpets, mirrors, NOS chrome, convertible
tops and trunk liners for postwar Cadillacs, with
a specialty of 1953-66 Eldorados.

Norman McIntosh
16401 West Seven Mile Road
Detroit, MI 48235
(313) 837-8835
Cadillac literature and parts, plus antique and
modern Cadillac limousine hire service.

Roy Sea
3030 N.E. 22nd Street
Fort Lauderdale, FL 33305
Parts and literature for 1954-56 Cadillacs.

E.J. Serafin
20 Hawthorne Avenue
Rockville Center, NY 11570
Reproduction owners and shop manuals for 1947
and 1949 models.

Solomon's, Inc.
544 East Main, Box 115
East Orwell, OH 44034
(216) 437-8622
Exhaust systems both new and used: also NOS.

RESTORATION
Listed below are only those shops stating a Cadillac specialty. Many other restoration shops are
equally competent to restore postwar Cadillacs,
and these generalists should also be consulted.

Cars & Parts of Yesteryear
Groveland Road, Box 151
Pipersville, PA 18947
(215) 297-5467

Classique Cars Unlimited
5 Turkey Bayou Road, PO Box 6
Lakeshore, MS 39558
(601) 467-9633

New York Classic Car Co.
2201 Town & Country Plaza
Cazenovia, NY 13035
(315) 655-8808

Index

Cadillac Models

Allanté,
  1987-93, 186-189
Calais,
  1965-70, 117-120,
  1971-76, 135-137,
Cimarron,
  1982-88, 168-170
DeVille,
  1959-60, 96-100,
  1961-64, 108-112,
  1965-70, 117-120,
  1971-76, 135-137,
  1977-84, 153-158,
  1985-93, 171-175
Eldorado Brougham,
  1957-58, 89-93,
  1959-60, 104-105,
  1961-66, 113-114,
Eldorado,
  1953, 56-61,
  1954-55, 67-70,
  1957-58, 86-88,
  1959-60, 101-103,
  1967-70, 126-132,
  1971-78, 141-146,
  1979-85, 159-161,
  1986-91, 179-182,
  1992-93, 183-185
Fleetwood,
  Seventy-Five 1968-76, 133-134,
  Seventy-Five 1985-87, 176-178
  Sixty-Special 1971-76, 138-140,
  Limousine 1977-84, 153-158,
  Brougham 1977-92, 153-158,

  1985-92, 171-175,
  1993, 153-158,
Seventy-Five,
  1946-49, 26-29,
  1950-53, 52-55,
  1954-67, 74-80,
  Fleetwood 1968-76, 133-134
Seville,
  1975-79, 141-152,
  1980-85, 162-167,
  1986-91, 179-182,
  1992-93, 183-185
Sixty-One,
  1946-47, 13-16,
  1948, 30-32,
  1949-51, 37-38,
Sixty-Special,
  1946-47, 23-25,
  1948, 35-36,
  1949-53, 47-51,
  1957-58, 94-95,
  1959-60, 106-107,
  1961-65, 115-116,
  1966-70, 121-125,
  Fleetwood Brougham 1971-76, 138-140,
  1987-93, 171-175
Sixty-Two,
  1946-47, 17-22,
  1948, 33-34,
  1949-53, 39-46,
  1954-56, 62-66,
  1957-58, 81-85,
  1959-60, 96-100,
  1961-64, 108-112,